BOATS YE'
SAILING

Trevor Boult

Foreword by Sophie Neville

Trevor Boult

Copyright © 2021 Trevor Boult. All rights reserved. ISBN 978-1-83808-457-8
The right of Trevor Boult to be identified as the author of this work has been asserted in accordance with the Copyright Act 1991.
Photographs and other images reproduced herein are © the author or from the author's collection except where credited otherwise.
No part of this publication may be reproduced, stored in a retrieval system or transmitted in any form or by any means, electronic, mechanical, photocopying, recording or otherwise, without prior permission in writing from the author.

CONTENTS

Quote & Dedication 3
Foreword 4
Fairhaven 5
Reflections of a Mirror 7
A Sea-Worthy Association: *Sir Winston Churchill* 21
Corryvreckan Spins Yarns 31
At Corryvreckan 37
Chilawee & *Chikanee*: Big Small & Little Small 39
Remembering Bligh and Shackleton 46
Boats Yet Sailing: The International Boatbuilding Training Centre 49
A Ranger and Shepherd go Forth 85
A Priceless Chippendale in Wroxham 88
Breezes on Bassenthwaite 92
Ketches of Character: The Ocean Youth Club 100
White Moth A-Broad 109
A Fleet Worth Hunting 114
A Delayed Date with *Christina* 118
Musings at the Moorings 122
Beyond the Bowsprit 123
Biographical Note 127

...To have touched the living treebark of larches
By the lakeside; and recalled their kind,
Long since fashioned by the same hand
Into planks of boats yet sailing.
Thank you, times past...

From: *Thank You,* by Trevor Boult

Dedication

To Master Jack – and to boats as yet un-sailed.

FOREWORD

by Sophie Neville

I have only launched one ship. When *Swallow*, the clinker-built dinghy featured in the original film *Swallows and Amazons* (1974) was fully renovated in 2011, I was invited up to Coniston Water in the Lake District, asked to slosh ginger wine over her bows and bless all those who hoped to sail her.

Books and boats go well together. Following tradition wrought by Arthur Ransome, I hereby bless Trevor Boult's *Boats Yet Sailing*. May it transport you through uncharted waters and across balmy seas, enabling you to live out adventures without getting your feet wet.

Trevor's voyages of discovery would have delighted the Swallows. He whisks you back to the joy of sailing over the bar in a brave little Mirror dinghy and forging bonds with family members while coping with steep launching ramps. Those of us who have grappled with a daggerboard and survived audacious currents after launching off a muddy beach can find solace in tales that take us to the Hebrides, Lindisfarne, Bassenthwaite, St Malo, and beyond. Dip into this book and you will be longing for the tinkling of halyards and the slapping sound of a loose jib, eager to take up the next offer to go sailing whatever the weather. I'd forgotten about the joy of singing sea shanties while rolling in on the tide, but memories of itchy Aran jerseys and early self-bailers bring back life in the 'seventies, when untangling a pulley system was part of growing up.

In 1930, Arthur Ransome used his royalties from *Swallows and Amazons*, or 'Spanish gold' as he put it, to buy a little yacht he called *Nancy Blackett*. Trevor has caught the vision by kindly donating royalties from this book to the Arthur Ransome Trust, the literacy charity Schoolreaders and The Arthur Ransome Society which provides young members with grants enabling them to learn to sail or take part in Ransomesque activities.

Sail back in time, taste salt on your tongue and take joy in the feel of wind in your hair. Ride the waves as the cries of gulls fill the air and wonder at the vastness of the Atlantic Ocean. Turning the pages of this memoir is like being in a dream, knowing that you could set sail yourself one day soon. May it inspire you to venture forth and fulfil your wildest imaginings.

FAIRHAVEN

Cullercoats: a small and historic fishing village on the northeast coast of England; it has always been a Fair Haven. Fronted by a compact semi-circular bay of fine golden sand, guarded by two ancient stone piers with a narrow entrance, which curls the moody advancing waves from the North Sea into a benign smile, it used to be home to a fleet of sailing cobles that supported the immediate fishing community. In the mid-1880s, it also became the temporary residence of one of America's greatest artists, Winslow Homer. His watercolour depictions of the fishing families and the cobles themselves not only changed his art from then on, but placed Cullercoats on the international map.

In the recent past, Cullercoats retained its harbour function as a haven for several motorized successors of the original cobles. Unique in functional design, and with a rare beauty of form, the remnant fleet of modern cobles continue to inspire not only artists, but the preservation of the sailing tradition on the home coasts, from Northumberland south to Yorkshire.

I am privileged to be a native of the environs of Cullercoats. I felt its wet sands oozing between my toddler toes whilst paddling; the gash of slimy rocks on shins during pre-teenage misadventures on the rocky foreshores adjacent to the bay; the struggles with perspective as a youth trying to accurately sketch the illusive beauty of the cobles drawn up on the boat stand, or afloat at their moorings; to successfully plead my way onto the cobles as they went to sea in the pre-dawns to attend lobster pots, or nets; and latterly, as a crusty professional mariner, to experience the thrill of being given the helm of a magnificent traditional sailing coble on a day of boisterous breezes and feel the pull and power of the taut tan sails overhead.

The family home of my upbringing was located a few streets back from the seafront. The house had no name, but eventually acquired one, chosen by my mother: Fairhaven. It owes its origin to a lake of that name at Lytham St. Annes, near Blackpool. The lake marked my childhood initiation into the practical world of boats and of sailing. During a family holiday on the west coast, my brother – three years my senior – and already a junior crew of a sailing dinghy whose owner raced weekly with the nearby Tynemouth Sailing Club, took charge of a small wooden craft for hire on Fairhaven Lake. As beginner crew I ducked my head and moved my weight where required, pulled dutifully on the controlling ropes of the foresail – evidently known as sheets, and jib – and eventually disembarked with a vital seed implanted in my mind which, perhaps, in the way of these things, led inevitably to a lifelong love of boats and the sea.

Where it all began for the author. He and his brother set sail in a hire boat at Fairhaven Lake, Lytham St. Annes.

REFLECTIONS OF A MIRROR

On departing Cullercoats harbour, keeping the two vertical white poles of the leading marks on the cliff top in line astern, to stay within the navigable channel between the outlying rocks, the cobles and other like craft intent on inshore fishing would variously turn either north- or southwards. The latter would see ahead, over a mile away, the dark line of the massive North Pier at the entrance to the River Tyne. It protrudes from a mighty headland; the end profile bears a striking resemblance to that of Queen Victoria and is thus referred to by locals. Unseen beyond its proud stature the little sandy bay of Priors Haven nestles hard beneath its cliffs which support the ancient ruins of Tynemouth Castle and Priory.

In a quiet corner of the haven, a fisherman's hut and a lone white coble – *Admiral* – used to shelter adjacent to the clubhouse of Tynemouth Sailing Club. *Admiral* became a subject for my camera, when a youth. Little did I know then that in a decade she would be the first coble I would set out to sea in, from her new home at Cullercoats. Before then, I became familiar with the many sailing dinghies which cluttered the beach, in their regular rows in front of the old wooden clubhouse.

Tynemouth Sailing Club was established during the late 1880s. At that time, the club boats were mostly centreboard canoes, yawl rigged with balanced lug sails. In the late 1960s, I became a junior member of the club and found myself a lightweight but nimble crew in a Mirror dinghy, the owner of which later became my brother's father-in-law: Joe Barratt. At this time the club raced four classes of dinghy: International 14s, Enterprises, National 12s and Mirrors. Sundays were the main race days with a winter season based upstream of Newcastle, on the river reaches at Ryton Willows. This offered a very different kind of close quarter racing in cold and confined waters, a change from the broad pier-embracing estuary at the river mouth, or occasionally on the open sea beyond.

The varnished cold-mould wooden hulls of the powerful International 14s with their crews outstretched on trapeze, the elegant clinker hulls of the nippy National 12s, the one-design classes of Enterprises and Mirrors; in whatever setting the distinct white blue and red sails, intermingling in separate competition, made a stirring Rule Britannia spectacle. It was an exciting world into which I was initiated, guided ably by Joe, who was imperturbable.

Co-designed in the early 1960s by Jack Holt and Barry Bucknall, the popular Mirror proved to be a robust and capable little racing dinghy. Their gunter rig, with jib, short mast and extending gaff which could be stowed within the hull's length, provided a worthwhile power plant for the stocky hull, with a freeboard capable of tackling the chops of the open sea inshore, along with the larger boats. They were raced as an end in themselves and not necessarily as a stepping stone. They could also be easily handled on and off a range of launching and landing situations, be carried on the roof of a car, or barely noticed when towed. Likewise, their stowage off site – even under the roof of a garage, as was to happen later with the family Mirror, the number of which – 15209 – remains emblazoned in the memory.

Imperviousness to cold seems a common quality of the young; likewise to wet, and vigorous exertion. The clothing I was advised to wear for my very first experience on a race day out from Priors Haven went on to serve me well for the ensuing years, with only seasonal adjustments. There were no wet- or dry-suits; soled 'wet-socks' were the only concession for the feet. Elsewhere, it was natural fibre products with an outer covering of lightweight Peter Storm waterproofs. Gloves were not a practical option. Later, the occasional dunking would result in the blue woollen Aran-pattern jumper knitted by my mother gaining more ground towards my knees.

Any pretext at being able to keep dry was dispelled on first launching off the beach. It has been said that if you can sail out and in at Priors Haven, you can do so anywhere. The immediate topography, both above and below water, linked with the varying states of the tides, and the ability of the wind to come from unexpected directions, could offer immediate challenges, before open water and a clear wind were reached. Having to hold the boat whilst the helmsman climbed in, I was often wet up to my thighs before I could embark. Sometimes, a lack of depth meant that the daggerboard which operated through the crew thwart, remained mostly raised, making further physical movement difficult.

This was a far cry from the genteel exclusiveness on Fairhaven Lake! As other craft of the motley armada took their places for launching, I was caught up in the nervous thrill of the event, careful to act on Joe's quietly spoken instructions. Afloat and with the jib sheet duly hauled, I kept my eye on the 'blind side', reporting anything which would be of interest to the helm. To port, the imposing granite bulk of the North Pier reared high above; the bluff headland of the Spanish Battery on the other side gave way to the sight of the broad estuary. The daggerboard was fully lowered; I moved towards the windward side in response to a sudden insistent heel. The sails, close-hauled, began to gently thrumb and our little craft leapt in lively fashion over the run of waves, which reached across the estuary from the direction of the great curving arm of the South Pier.

REFLECTIONS OF A MIRROR

In the well of the boat, running fore and aft from the central thwart, loose webbing straps were pointed out to me. Invited to sit on the weather gunwale next to Joe, keeping my weight pressed forward next to the mast's wire stay – or shroud – and my feet tucked under the toe-straps, I found myself leaning out in concert with Joe, at the next gust of wind. The boat

The River Tyne estuary: principal racing venue for Tynemouth Sailing Club.

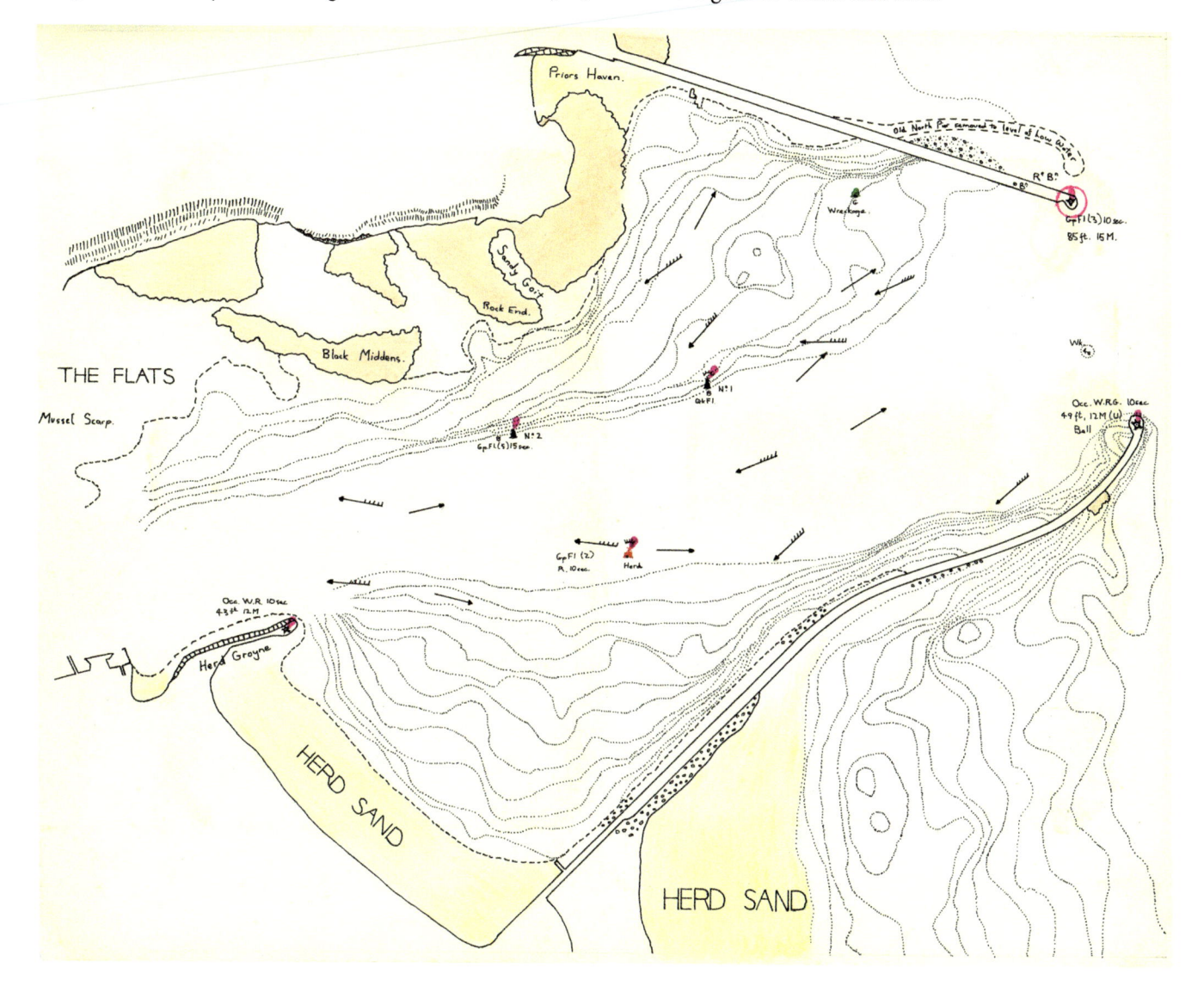

9

responded, as did I – with exhilaration! I was reminded of the pre-tacking instructions of 'Ready about' – then 'Lee-ho!' – having a training session on the way towards the race starting line. Efficient tacking was not only one of the key elements in racing, but best practice for any style of sailing. In the time before the Mirror fleet was summoned by the ten minute gun, I had learned the technique of briefly holding the jib until 'backed' by the wind, to encourage the bow to continue turning through the eye of the wind, before rapidly letting the sheet fly, and hauling aggressively on the new sheet through the 'cam cleat' which then held it taut and secure.

The Committee boat was moored at one end of the starting line which ran roughly at right-angles to the direction of the wind, such that the first leg of the race would be 'upwind'. On the boat's signal mast, various flags and burgees fluttered, potent symbols of elapsing time, and the class of boat which was next in line to start. When the time came for the Mirror fleet, jockeying for the best position in the run up to the starting 'gun' saw much manoeuvring, the spilling of wind, and bunching near the 'upwind' marker buoy, where being on starboard tack would give tactical advantage. Stopwatches were scrutinized; eyes fixed on the Committee boat flags. A countdown of seconds was made, until the blare of the horn and the lowering of the start flag signalled the beginning of the race.

Joe had manoeuvred well: we crossed the line close to the buoy, having sped up to it on a reach before turning to windward and hauling in the sheets. It was a brisk but fair breeze and the tension of the pre-start gave way to making the most of the wind, of deciding when to tack and carrying out manoeuvres efficiently and without undue haste so as to minimize the loss of forward motion. When on port tack we duly gave way to those we encountered on starboard tack: and kept stoically on that tack when the reverse applied: ready to hail STARBOARD! should our opponent decide not to see us!

From the crowding at the start, the boats spread out as they each raced for the windward mark, choosing to make use of local gusts or indeed calmer stretches to change tack, deciding when to tack so as to make a chosen location, making canny allowance for the sideways drift of 'leeway', which is a by-product of trying to claw upwind.

Rounding the mark brought a dramatic change in apparent conditions. It was now the 'downwind' leg where the boats run with the wind astern. Suddenly, the wind on the face had gone; likewise the heeling of the boat, the slap of waves and the thrumb of the taut sails. In their place was a gentle breeze caressing the back of the neck, the easy scending motion of the hull and the run of waves keeping pace with us. The purpose of the sails changes from that of an aircraft wing to that of a barn door, maximizing the area for the wind to blow us downwind.

The mainsail sheet was eased out until the boom rested against the mast's shroud; the jib was likewise loosened. When the wind was right astern, the jib was hauled clear of the mainsail – a condition known as goosewinging. The daggerboard was not needed and was raised to cut down on drag, and the lifting rudder blade was also partially raised.

Goosewinging is a condition which needs careful monitoring. I had yet to learn the manoeuvre of gybing – passing the stern through the wind (not passing wind by the stern!) – and its inherent dangers. If the following wind gets 'behind' the mainsail it can cause it to sweep across the boat. The rapidly moving boom could hit crew on the head, the long length of mainsheet could snag and the resultant rocking of the boat could briefly render instability a reality.

On this day the downwind marker was provided by the local authorities. Near the end of the North Pier a conical green buoy emblazoned with a large white W officially marked the position of a wreck. Seen only from the high vantage of the promenade on the pier itself, its true size came as a shock, as it loomed large. Rounding a downwind mark also has its racing techniques. If approaching boats are bunching, the wind might be 'stolen' from a boat ahead; if a boat is overhauled before two boat lengths from the mark, the cry of WATER AT THE MARK! secures the inner boat's priority. The marker should also be rounded so as to minimize the loss of ground downwind.

The final leg of the triangular course allowed for the 'fastest point of sailing' – that of reaching. Here, the final destination can be reached without the need for tacking and in such a manner that the set of the sails can achieve the fastest movement of the boat. On this day, I was to be shown by Joe how some of the bigger boats, especially the International 14s, were able to get onto 'the plane', where the wind strength was such that the boats lost their full displacement and with the crews' weight moved well aft, they appeared almost to take off across the water.

The first round of the course was followed by a repeat. At this stage, it was possible to assess how we were placed and, in the changing conditions of the wind, tidal sets and river current in the wide estuary, tactics were discussed and considered anew. Joe burst into song with a fine rendition of 'O Solo Mio': in what turned out to be a signature expression of the fun he was having. We did not win the Mirror race but showed a creditable performance: hopefully not too much hindered by this novice. There was still packed lunch to have ashore before the afternoon race. At its conclusion, the boat was parked along with the others in its row of summer storage on the beach front behind a protective barrier of locally sourced sea rocks; a warming shower at the clubhouse before cycling home. I joined my brother as reluctant

Opposite: Sailing their own Mirror dinghy on a family holiday in North Wales: here seen in Colwyn Bay, August 1969.

choristers, press-ganged into the choir by our organist & choirmaster father at the local Parish Church; exchanging waterproofs, buoyancy aids and ruddy complexions for cassocks, ruffs and cherubic expressions; and not to sing 'O Solo Mio', but the strains of choral evensong.

*

As the main sailing season at the coast ended, racing was to continue throughout the maturing autumn and winter months, from the south bank of the River Tyne, well upstream from Newcastle itself, at the rural setting of Ryton Willows. Joe's boat was recovered from the beach and stored in the double garage of his home in Tynemouth. The boat was towed to and from Ryton on race days, a journey of some fifteen miles, initially by dual carriageway, and the through ways to the west of the city. His classic dark blue and curvaceous Volvo saloon was to be seen in the fast lane, thundering westwards, with Mirror in tow, to the sound of radio music. Joe's tapping fingers drummed accompanying percussion on the steering wheel. An enduring memory was the hit single at the time, *Sugar sugar* …

The approach to the river at Ryton is by a tortuous and very steeply dropping lane through woodland, before crossing the railway line which links Newcastle with Carlisle, in order to use a sloping stone ramp into the upper tidal reach. This runs in a gentle east-west arc for over a mile; bounded by upstream shallows and by a bridge downstream. A small fenced-in boat-park was used by some as storage. At a time when winters produced copious and lingering snow, owners could arrive to see the canvas covers of their boats rigid and pooled with ice. The access lane, too, provided added interest in such times: vehicles with gallant assistants sitting on bonnets to encourage upward traction were not unknown.

*

Our parents were always supportive of our interests. Their response to the request from my brother and me to acquire a second-hand Mirror dinghy of our own was positive. A suitable craft was located locally and the family car, an elegant two-tone Singer Vogue with gleaming chrome, sprouted an incongruous roof rack. The white, upturned hull of the boat sat neatly above the curved pillar box red of the car roof, the boom, short wooden mast and more lengthy gaff nestling alongside, whilst rudder, tiller, sail bag and canvas cover occupied the boot. Father drove gingerly back to the sailing club at Tynemouth. An unusual launching trolley with rigid blue buoyant wheels completed the ensemble. Thus Mirror 15209 – the sail number – became our proud possession: we had big plans. The boat was named *Trevian 1,* a mix of our two forenames, and acknowledging already that there might be a Number 2 at some future date.

Summer holidays were in the offing: a week in North Wales, self-catering at Gwrych Castle – an extraordinary replica medieval pile near the coastal town of Abergele: the Mirror, and launching trolley, came too. The beaches at Colwyn Bay provided excellent sea sailing, whilst the enclosed central Menai Straits offered navigational challenges amidst the grand enclosing scenery of either bank. Here, we nearly came to minor grief: a lesson about gybing. Always keen to practise sailing technique, we selected a little mooring float to round whilst executing a gybe. Unfortunately, the droop of the long doubled length of the main sheet snagged the top of the buoy, effectively tethering us. We were travelling at some speed: the effect was a sudden stop and the prospect of capsize, which was narrowly averted. Lesson learned.

As the Lake District was another favoured holiday location, *Trevian 1* also took to Windermere and Ullswater, launching from the roadside at Glencoyne, famous for Wordsworth's inspiration for his poem, *Daffodils*.

At the end of this season, responding to an observation that some of the 'stitch-and-glue' joints around the daggerboard and inner side panels were leaking, we decided on a remedy: reinforcement, by applying more fibreglass resin and tape. In each of the main buoyancy spaces a large circular hole was cut, to accept a proprietary watertight inspection hatch. This enabled access to the blind side of the weeping joints. The results of our weight-adding efforts made the boat an excellent heavy weather racer, but less so in light airs. We knew where our priority lay!

Gadgets were also appealing and in this we were lucky. There was a major outlet for specialist sailing paraphernalia on the outskirts of Newcastle: Fox & Hounds. Our mode of transport on a Saturday morning was always a high speed pedalling on our racing bikes, using the major roads of half a century ago. Teenage freedoms, and the concerns of parents, were of a different order then.

In the course of several visits, interspersed by DIY activities on the boat at the Club, we installed a self-bailer: a stainless steel device set into the floor of the hull, which, when lowered during forward movement, sucked out shipped water through a non-return flap. To make fine adjustments to the shape of the mainsail, a 'tack downhaul' and 'clew outhaul' were fitted to the fore- and aft-ends of the boom, with handily located quick-fastening jamb cleats. These allowed the sail to be flattened during strong winds and eased to give more shape to the sail during zephyrs. A kicking strap was fitted to the inner end of the boom, which holds the boom horizontally when the sail is eased out for more efficient sailing during downwind passages. To either side of the mast a pair of clip cleats accepted an aluminium jib pole, used to hold the clew of the jib when goosewinging. We decided not to invest in a spinnaker and chute: we were

Launching *Trevian 1* at Prior's Haven, Tynemouth: captured on a postcard.

not that fanatical! A change of image was also acted upon: the hull was painted bright red and the transom which had been painted white was stripped and varnished. I revelled in painting the boat's name in gothic style lettering.

As autumn took hold and with it the close of the racing season at the mouth of the Tyne, we had to think about proper all-weather storage. For the first winter we took advantage of the free boat-park at the winter sailing location at Ryton, utilizing our historic lift on the rear seat of Joe's Volvo. Despite being extra careful in bracing the heavy cover against ingress of rainwater, it was not uncommon to find frozen ovals weighing down the board-like canvas. Only the brave, or eccentric, took to the water to race in such conditions: like we did!

In the single garage at the family home, with its wide wooden doors and heavily braced

Ryton Open Meeting, October 1969, start of 2nd race. 15209 on starboard tack, upwind; in the lead. Result 15209 came second.

flat roof, a pulley system and wooden beams were set up in order for the boat to be hoisted for all-weather storage. A local chandlers at North Shields Fish Quay, stocked for the needs of the local fleet, provided what turned out to be galvanized blocks which would have lifted a trawler's bloated cod-end aboard, let alone lift a 120 pound Mirror dinghy!

*

The return to Tynemouth was a marker for the passage of time, as we embarked on another racing season. I generally acted as crew with my elder brother helming: but we occasionally swapped roles. By this time my brother had reached his stature of 6′ 4″, requiring deftness and dexterity in such confined space. During Open Meetings – races where other clubs took part – we would rub the hull over with fine wet-and-dry cloth: an activity carried out regularly by the keenest Mirror owner, a young woman from Ireland who took her racing – and her winning – very seriously. Open meetings, and indeed the occasional National and World championship in some of the classes, were generally held at sea, beyond the estuary and piers, in open waters away from commercial traffic, to cancel any tactical advantages of local knowledge by those whose home waters these were.

The Mirror dinghy is capable of sailing in coastal waters. The freeboard of the hull, which makes it appear stubby, also makes it as dry a boat as the larger Enterprise. On a non-race day in summer, weather conditions were perfect for using our boat for a small local cruise: northwards and into the charming sandy bay and harbour at Cullercoats. It was to be a unique event, and provided a fresh viewpoint of the home coast. It was also a precursor to my later early morning voyages from Cullercoats, aboard a working coble engaged on attending fleets of lobster pots or trammel nets. As if to continue the theme, we next sailed up river, passing the bustling Fish Quay and the reach where shipyards abounded, rounding the great curve by Tyne Commission Quay where the liners to Norway berthed, and opposite Tyne Dock, entry point for the coal and iron ore hauled by the latest and most powerful British steam locomotives made, to reach the heights of Consett Iron Company nine hundred feet up in the hills of Durham. Feeling suddenly small and vulnerable we took to mid channel and the now ebbing tidal stream back to 'safety'!

At the mouth of the river proper lies a notorious grouping of rocks known as the Black Middens; site of many an historic shipwreck, so much so that an early lifeboat house was situated on the adjacent shore. It rises exposed at low tide. Between this broad curving expanse and the foreshore lies a channel of deeper water. Choosing a quiet day, my brother and I used the Mirror as a rowing dinghy in order to 'survey' this channel. Using the aluminium jib-pole as a sounding rod we probed the channel to see if it could be used as a 'short cut' during races.

Unsure as to the results, or indeed the ethics, we never acted on our findings.

The Mirror was also used as a dive support vessel and, as it turned out, something of a rescue boat. Now at a polytechnic, my brother had joined a club and become proficient in sub-aqua diving. An inaugural local dive was made in the estuary, as he slipped over the boat's stern. I was informed of the visual signals: a steady raised hand signalled 'okay': a waving hand is for summoning assistance. The dive was going smoothly until some while later I observed a dark bobbing head – and a frantically waving arm. Bending to the oars, on regaining the boat over the stern, I learned that cramps had gripped the calves of both legs: more lessons learned.

Racing in virtual calms requires a different set of skills. In order to keep the sails 'filled' and in shape, as opposed to flapping uselessly, our 'weight' was disposed on the leeside, deliberately causing the boat to heel over. Physical movements and those of the helm were made gently. It even seemed correct to be whispering. Every nuance of the wind was responded to, the sea surface scrutinized for the signs of a cat's paw of breeze, or the oiliness of utter calm. At the head of the gaff a burgee indicated the apparent breeze but attached to the shrouds, at eye level, a long sliver of old nylon stocking gave hint of zephyrs. Particular attention also needed to be given to the commercial buoyed channel into the river. Colliers and ferries could suddenly appear, either from seaward or around the obscuring upriver bend. The safety boats would be on hand to marshal the dinghies not to risk crossing the channel. On occasion, some would do so, prompting the disapproving five-short-blasts on the transiting ship's whistle.

More often than not there was not only a working breeze but the prospect of excess. At the Coastguard station on the high bluff behind the clubhouse, the hoisted black cone denoting the imminence of either a northerly, or southerly gale, indicated an exciting day ahead. On such occasions, even the Mirror could be coaxed onto a plane. It could also stretch the boat's spars beyond endurance. Taking to the water, with Joe invited to be at the helm once more, we were battling upwind on an exhilarating 'beat' when, in an instant, a resounding CRACK and mayhem left us in sudden quiet and a tangle of sail, and ropes: the stubby wooden mast had snapped. With typical *sang froid*, it was remarked that 'something mast have broken!' The club's safety boat towed us back to shore. The incident was not a costly one: the short and simple wooden mast was easily replaced.

*

Sailing can rightly be described not only as a past-time but, thankfully, as a sport. It was to the latter description that I was able to convince the sports department at Tynemouth 6th Form College to allow me to take the Mirror out into the estuary for an afternoon's sailing with a friend, as opposed to engaging in team sports on the playing fields. Yet again, this is a reflection

BOATS YET SAILING

Outside Fairhaven, in later life, the Mirror is readied for a long road journey south to Market Harborough in Leicestershire, and new owners.

of the 'can do' spirit of the times, both for students and college staff, where risk and trust were not only considered but allowed. It was a privilege we respected. Sailing solo in these waters did need care and the college never had cause to regret their consent.

However, we did indulge in slight mischief. The massive North Pier has a walkway set on the seaward side, with a lower level facing the estuary. At low tide it is possible in certain winds to sail beyond sight of the walkway. On one occasion, thrashing towards the pier close-hauled, we tacked at the last moment to re-appear eventually further upwind. We could not help notice a knot of concerned walkers poised at the rails, seemingly convinced of our collision and demise.

Visual impressions can take other forms. The visit of two relatives from Ireland prompted the suggestion of a sail with the husband. It was a completely new experience for him and one which had evidently stirred previously dormant Horatio Nelson genes. Driving home afterwards, with a three course lunch in prospect, he continued to wear the bright red buoyancy waistcoat at the dinner table and all through the repast. Apparently it was 'him'…

The lounge in the clubhouse at Tynemouth Sailing Club was eventually used as the social

A rigging demonstration for friend and new owner, Malcolm Lewis, in the garden of his home.

venue following the marriage of my brother and his wife. As best man and a cadet officer in the Merchant Navy, I rather nervously sported my uniform and delivered my speech without too many gaffs. The father of the bride, my sailing mentor, Joe, delivered a master class in the art of such speaking, taking instant advantage of circumstances. At this time the Swan Hunter shipyard at Wallsend had been building a series of what were dubbed 'super tankers', 250,000-ton Very Large Crude Carriers: monsters the like of which had never been seen before. Their launch and eventual departure from the Tyne were major spectacles. As Joe was concluding his pithy speech he happened to see over the shoulders of the guests, out through the panoramic windows which faced the pier ends, the latest super tanker appear from behind the bluff headland known as The Spanish Battery. Indicating that he had spared no expense for his daughter's wedding, he invited the throng to turn and observe his finale, which, right on time, was dwarfing the seaward vista.

*

I bought my first car second-hand from my parents: a trusty VW Polo. A new arrangement for transporting the Mirror dinghy needed to be found and I invested in a custom road trailer. A nearby friend had a disused spare garage which enabled storage at very reasonable rates. On acquiring my own first house, on the outskirts of Berwick-upon-Tweed, a rather ramshackle wooden double garage took over the task. Accessed down a lengthy side driveway, I took the opportunity to self-learn reversing with a trailer. I seemed to pick up the knack and indeed relished the manoeuvre.

Actual use of the boat inevitably dwindled, but boat and trailer came with me to the East Neuk of Fife when I relocated five years later to the picturesque coastal village of St Monans. Boat and trailer were hoisted into the storage loft of nearby Elie Sailing Club, reappearing eighteen months later for a return to Tyneside. A final long-haul journey to Market Harborough in Leicestershire, to the home of a friend and fellow student at the International Boatbuilding Training Centre in Suffolk, finally saw '15209' change hands. The boat eventually was gifted to the Sea Scouts at Fishguard in Wales.

It is in the memory, the wintry river reaches of the Tyne, in the estuary mouth and on the beach at Priors Haven that the spirit of '15209' lingers: captured on a postcard of the bay, as a lone little 'red boat' bravely setting out from shore.

A SEA-WORTHY ASSOCIATION: SIR WINSTON CHURCHILL

As a dexterous teenager, I had revelled in the construction of several plastic models of classic sailing ships – HMS *Victory*, *Cutty Sark* and the Boston Whaler, *Charles W Morgan*, the last of which remains to this day, sealed in a home-made display case and kept well away from the spar-bending influence of the sun's rays. Amongst other things, these models introduced me to the mysterious nomenclature of sailing ships: the names of masts, yards, sails and rigging were devoured eagerly.

I learned from accompanying literature the strengths and weaknesses of how these vessels functioned at sea. The operation of a square-rigger was complex and very much governed and restricted by wind direction. Fore-and-aft rigged vessels, like ketches and larger schooners were able to claw their way in the direction of the wind much more effectively. My attention, therefore, was directed to another such vessel that might offer the kind of experiences which would satisfy these interests.

Already a cadet in the Merchant Navy, I was aware of the two impressive sail training schooners, *Sir Winston Churchill* and *Malcolm Miller*. Always supportive of the endeavours of both my brother and me, my parents kindly sponsored this latest adventure, which enabled me to sail as a trainee on *Sir Winston Churchill*: her inspirational name, of course, was irresistible!

*

Having been a cadet for nearly two years and completed the first of two lengthy stints ashore attending South Shields Marine College as a live-in student, which qualified me for 'remission of sea time' towards attaining my first professional qualification, I had become used to making journeys to join and leave ships in different UK ports, and to the confines of sharing an attic room with several other fellow cadets.

On this occasion, joining *Sir Winston Churchill* in Weymouth induced added excitement, mixed, as ever, with that of nervous expectation. 'Character building', promoted by the Sail Training Association as a key facet of their ethos, could be an intimidating phrase. With

Opposite: A bulkhead in the officers' wardroom testified to warm welcomes in many ports.

belongings stuffed into a large and collapsible canvas rucksack, I felt suitably equipped and apparelled as a Jolly Jack, off for a stint 'Before the Mast'!

At the riverside berth in Weymouth, opposite Custom House Quay, nestling amongst the charming buildings of the town, the setting seemed aptly historic and to scale. The topsail schooner's three masts reared skywards, the crossed yards of her foremast at a precise right-angle. *Sir Winston Churchill* looked awesomely impressive and thoroughly shipshape. I was no longer intimidated by the aspect of a gangway leading onto an unknown vessel. Not a complete beginner to such a scene, at twenty years of age I was one of the more senior of the trainees. Likewise, integrating into the confined environment below decks with my fellows in dormitory-style accommodation, where most aspects of socializing were done in communal proximity. I looked forward to that experience with somewhat mixed feelings. As with any such assemblage, formal greetings were made by the Master; introductions made of the ship's staff; the trainees divided into watches; a tour made both below and above decks; the manner of operating the 'heads' and seamanlike conduct on the open decks. The first meal provided an early opportunity to break the ice with those sitting close by.

On deck, there was a bewildering array of rigging and ropes galore, rails of belaying pins and sundry mysterious tackle to trip over and massive wooden booms with expanses of neatly stowed sails constrained by regimented rows of reef-knotted rope gaskets.

The following day would normally have heralded departure for sea but, as the weather offshore was gearing up for a gale, time was spent on deck familiarization and training, and even some visits to the squared yards above. Hands gripped tightly, as the rope ratlines felt the tentative touch of be-plimsoled feet and the security of the deck gave way to the heady exposure of increasing height. Hauling sail was a manual affair, on the grounds that, literally, many hands make things work; another technique which relies heavily on team work. The large forestaysail was hoisted as an example. The appropriate belayed halyard on the fife rail was identified; the hauling team organized into a line down the deck; the instruction given to the first person on the halyard, who would be responsible for making up the tensioned rope around the belaying pin, having to utter the two commands to the rest of the team behind: 'get ready to come up' … 'COME UP!'

A rhythmic shanty-beat call of 'heave … heave … heave' saw the large triangular sail raised up the angled forestay, fluttering to the feel of a slight breeze. When the rope became taut, the response to 'COME UP!' saw all the haulers but the first let the rope go. At this instant the remaining trainee quickly took a couple of turns of the halyard around the belaying pin. 'Sweating up' was the next process. The taut halyard above the belaying pin was grasped and

A SEA-WORTHY ASSOCIATION: SIR WINSTON CHURCHILL

Opposite: A different kind of yard exercise: a lofty view from the foremast.

by pulling outwards bodily, any residual slack was rapidly taken up around the belaying pin before the halyard was secured with figure-of-eight turns, and the tail of the rope coiled neatly. On eventual departure, I found myself at the 'come up' position: unwittingly, it was to prove a painful and disabling event.

Departure occurred in the early afternoon of 19th October 1976. Before the schooner had even cleared the harbour entrance some sail had been raised. Considering myself an experienced forestaysail'man, I took up my position and, with enthusiasm, the team sent the sail skyward. The critical moment came: I hollered out the instruction 'Get ready to come up', then 'COME UP!' An instant later, a searing pain accompanied by the sensation of a twang in the knee of my forward-braced leg, gave me an unexpected 'character-building' moment. My instinct was to let the rope go, grab my knee and make some form of suitably nautical exclamation. I delayed this, choosing instead to get the halyard belayed before retiring from the forefront of operations. In the quiet of the wardroom my injury was assessed. Already swelling considerably, some damage to a ligament was diagnosed. Salve was applied and the knee bandaged. My limp would last for the whole voyage; my ability to go aloft restricted; and sleep was a disturbed affair. My fellows took my fortitude as a measure of heroism. I accepted it modestly …!

In light airs, more sail was made and then passage set southwards. Our first intended port of call was St. Malo, the historic walled city on the Emerald Coast of Brittany. The ship's transition into a living, moving entity on the high seas was clearly an enthralling one for many of the raw trainees, and no less so for me. The kindly Bosun and his mate were efficiency themselves, in motivating and guiding the new crew. By the helm, the stern visage of the captain probed ahead as he kept an additional eye on the trainee at the large spoked wooden wheel. He had an expression of stoic concentration on his face as he grappled with the mysteries of the magnetic compass. Astern, the home coasts diminished in scale and detail. The wind from the west became more certain and the schooner responded, giving the trainees the first feel of the unseen hand above which, in the mass of taut canvas, pulled *Sir Winston Churchill* through the water: a sensation very different to the sluggish push of a submerged propeller at the stern. There was a sense of voyaging: an overnight passage across busy marine highways; of watches on deck and below; of a dawn in the region of the Channel Islands and a port call in France.

By midnight, mid-Channel, the wind was strong and the schooner's motion lively in a corresponding sea. Consuming breakfast was an education. The group already had a shared and novel experience: not only a night-time afloat in boisterous conditions, but before the mast on a schooner of renown! The noon position on the chart put us to the south of Guernsey,

A SEA-WORTHY ASSOCIATION: SIR WINSTON CHURCHILL

having passed the island well to the west. We had been told that the seas surrounding the Channel Islands and indeed the adjacent mainland coasts were subject to fierce tidal streams and 'races'; careful navigation was vital. This intelligence added extra spice to our adventure.

Throughout the afternoon the westerly wind moderated and brought us to St. Malo shortly before sunset. The tall slender spire of the cathedral was like a beckoning finger; the substantial city walls and defensive bastion were an impressive sight in the fading light. The urge to explore had to be put on hold. There was the matter of stowing heavy sails in proper fashion, neatly on their booms and tidying below decks. In the still of evening there was the thrill of stepping onto an unknown foreign shore, after working a passage. A mental note was made to be careful crossing the roads, looking firstly to the left; of resurrecting school-French and the satisfaction of actually recognizing shop words and names of roads.

The following day, chores aboard ship continued. Brasswork was brightened after the excesses of the Channel crossing; we were introduced to 'Bibles' and 'prayer books', the large and smaller holystones historically used to whiten the teak decks. We felt we had earned our time off to further explore ashore. It was to be an early start the next day.

The logbook indicated departure at 0700; our intended destination was the Isles of Scilly. By midnight we had covered some ninety miles on a comfortable broad reach in moderate conditions. In the early hours a veering wind rose towards a gale. By noon a decision had been made not to make any more 'westing' and to ride the weather in more comfort. Like a naval frigate patrolling a picket line in the Western Approaches, the schooner traversed south and north to seaward of the tip of the Cornish Peninsula, before breaking off and heading for a destination synonymous with the sea and famous for its deep natural harbour: Falmouth!

Stepping ashore with other crew members at Custom House Quay, ringed with its mix of whitewashed historic buildings, after

Pulling well down Channel: getting to know the ropes – and trip hazards – was an education.

A SEA-WORTHY ASSOCIATION: SIR WINSTON CHURCHILL

Keeping shipshape: the author getting up close and personal with the 'dolphin striker', beneath the bowsprit.

two full nights at sea and now a second port call, there was the feeling of a team that was beginning to gel. Aspects of shipboard life, complicated by being a *bona fide* Tall Ship, were becoming more familiar and enjoyable; the treat and sense of freedom of 'going shoreside' was really appreciated.

The town streets were, in later years, to become like a second home, as I stood by a ship in drydock, then helping to care-take two vessels in layup. Local walks became familiar, as was my presence in the local library which I was able to join.

It was mid-afternoon the following day that we bade farewell to Falmouth and, after heading southwards to clear traffic lanes, turned eastwards in a moderate reaching wind towards the Channel Island of Alderney, which was attained shortly after midnight on 27th October.

Blessed with fine and settled weather, the chance to explore one of the lesser-populated and smaller islands of the archipelago was also taken. Such explorations were encouraged and needed no prompting: the prospect of discovery was ever a potent motive. I was not disappointed. On a sea-washed beach of golden sand, sitting perkily upright on her twin draughts, was a large coble – a symbol of home – and a long way from her own native coast of Northumberland. Clearly her owner appreciated the beach launching capabilities for which the coble design evolved. Taking to the schooner's small work boat, a fellow trainee and I spent a pleasant afternoon beneath the bowsprit's dolphin catcher, a tin

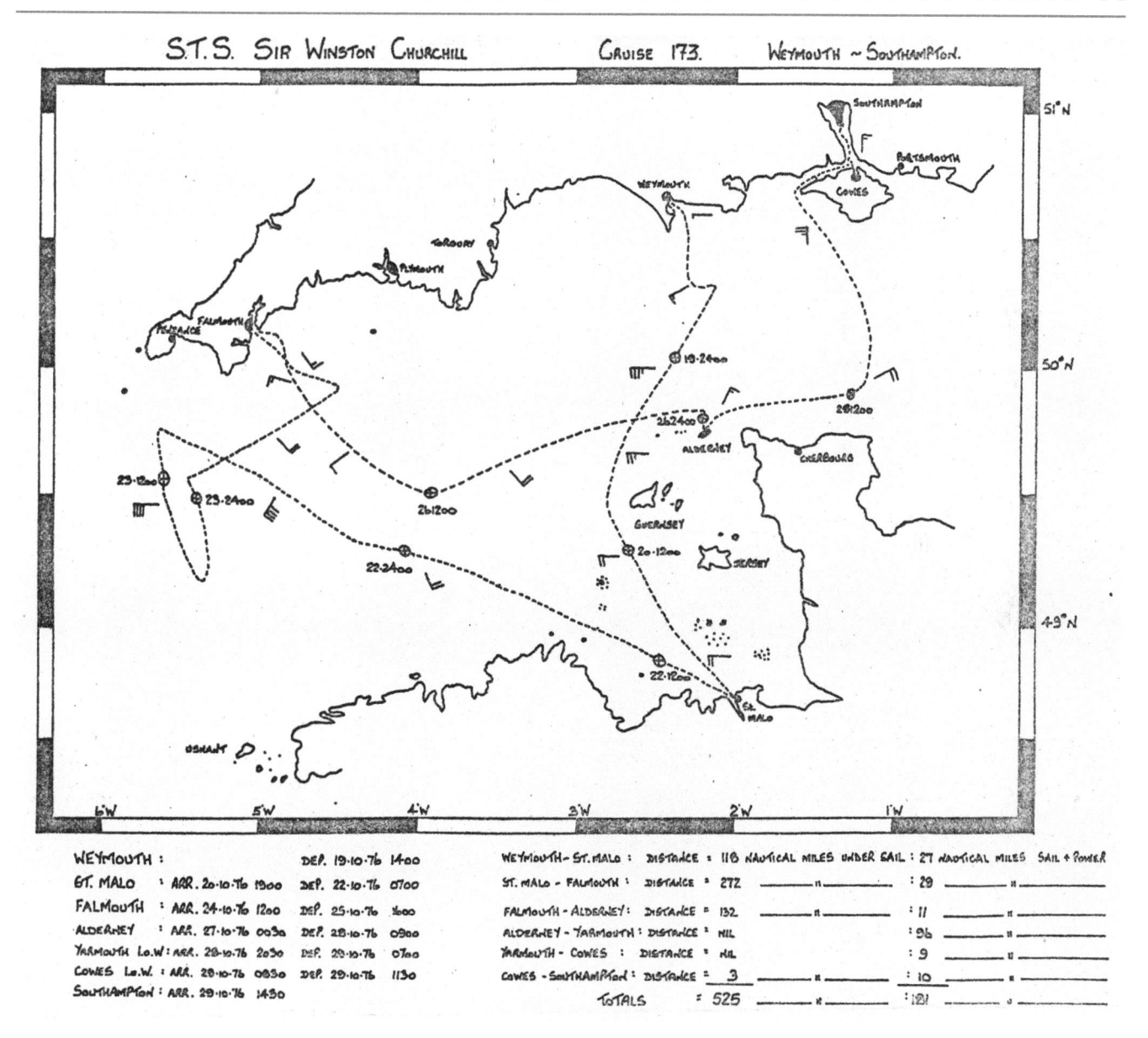

A SEA-WORTHY ASSOCIATION: SIR WINSTON CHURCHILL

Route of the Sail Training Schooner *Sir Winston Churchill*, in the western English Channel.

A young man and the sea…

of gloss white paint in the bilges, as we spruced up this disturbingly-named spar and its standing rigging.

We departed from Alderney during the morning of the penultimate day of the cruise, continuing up-Channel until beyond Cherbourg where, at noon, with the wind unusually from the east, a northerly heading placed our landfall at the western extremity of the Isle of Wight. Once again, the sighting of yet more famous nautical locations fuelled anticipation: the Needles; the Solent; Cowes; Spithead; Southampton Water. All were to figure as a fitting climax.

Like a row of blunt and stubby molars, the chalk stacks of the Needles, with their attendant dramatic lighthouse, were a spectacular welcome to home waters; likewise the passage in the Solent to Cowes, mecca of sailing and home to the Royal Yacht Squadron. In the roads, *Sir Winston Churchill* was brought up to anchor, to prepare for arrival at Southampton. The schooner logged a total distance of 706 nautical miles; 525 of which were under sail alone, the remainder being engine assisted.

Throughout the cruise, I had made light of my gradually deflating balloon-knee, which was tightly wrapped in bandages and periodically doused with deep-heat spray. My limp had given me a piratical gait and it was a pleasure to be selected by the Captain to take the helm for the passage up Southampton Water to the berth. A seasoned hand from my ongoing cadetship in the Merchant Navy, it was a novel extension of experience, to be at the wheel of the schooner for her graceful transit to Southampton.

Here, as is the way of these things, the bond of shared experience, the fellowship of the trainees and the association with the Captain, his watchkeepers and crew, dispersed at the gangway; but would not be forgotten: perhaps most of all the internal discoveries we each had made about ourselves.

CORRYVRECKAN SPINS YARNS

Corryvreckan! – a name that disturbs and stirs the imagination. A famous maelstrom which gives its title to the strait in which it inhabits – the Gulf of Corryvreckan – between the Scottish islands of Jura and Scarba, it is one of innumerable features which make the West Coast of Scotland one of the choice sailing grounds of the adventurous.

Having recently become a certificated junior officer in the Merchant Navy, on leave as Third Officer with the oceanographic ships of the Natural Environment Research Council, and in search of such adventure with a school friend, the name of a yacht, *Corryvreckan,* leapt out of the page of adverts for sailing holidays: it was indeed the deciding factor!

Experienced in racing sailing dinghies, and more recently as a trainee on a three-masted schooner, there was an evident gap which I felt needed filling: to cruise on a powerful ketch. Where better to do so than on Scotland's island-bejewelled west coast. *Corryvreckan* also did not disappoint.

Excitedly pouring over a map that exuded adventure-in-the-making, we located the home base of the yacht: Balvicar, on the isle of Seil. With the ease of youth, Tony and I went on to plan and carry out our lengthy journey from Tyneside to Argyll. Nearing journey's end, at Clachan we drove over a high-arched stone bridge across a narrow sea channel onto the island. We knew this to be the famous 'Bridge across the Atlantic'. Balvicar nestled in a sheltered bay of the same name on the east of Seil. In its tranquil waters, bathed by evening sunlight the yacht, recognized from it publicity photograph, lay contentedly at her mooring.

Our companions for the trip assembled with us on the jetty at the appointed hour, where we were courteously met by our skipper, sporting a magnificent beard. Tendered out to *Corryvreckan*, we were soon allocated berths and earnestly instructed on the functioning of the heads. Over an evening meal we got to know something of our fellow crew, the skipper and the boat.

The fine ferro-cement ketch, *Corryvreckan*, at her home port of Balvicar, Isle of Seil, in Western Scotland.

A former seagoing engineer, skipper Ken went on to reveal an arresting and admiring fact: he had built *Corryvreckan* himself. When first using Balvicar as home base, whilst occupying the owner's cabin aft, he had heard an inquisitive knocking on the hull. It transpired that it was made surreptitiously by bemused locals who had found out a strange fact about the yacht: the hull was made with ferro-cement.

The fact also caused us to poise our forkfuls of dinner in mid-air; a satisfying result for the amused teller of the tale. Ken then went on to enlighten us as to the concept, practicalities and advantages of building such a hull; also some of the potential problems.

We severally took to our bunks and were set for our adventure to start the next morning. Weather conditions were ideal. The chart of the area showed a glorious complex of islands, channels and skerries, all with romantically sounding names. On the rack above, well thumbed reference books indicated a reassuring thoroughness of the subject, the thick hardbound volume of the Clyde Cruising Club Sailing Directions for the West Coast of Scotland promising delicious perusal.

A fine start: southbound, exiting Seil Sound.

Heading south down Seil Sound, passing to the east of the island of Shuna, keeping close to the mainland shore we were yet aware that towards the west a brooding bulk of an island – Scarba – was the sentinel gate to our yacht's namesake: the Gulf of Corryvreckan! To its south the lower long flank of Jura was also a mystical island, its famous mountain 'Paps' another dramatic feature to anticipate as the day progressed. A steady breeze bore us down the length of the widening Sound of Jura. Lying off the west coast of Kintyre, the low-lying island of Gigha provided a sheltered anchorage for the night, in Ardminish Bay: a run ashore to visit a local hostelry was yet another agreeable facet of this style of cruising.

The following morning we backtracked, rounding Gigha before heading towards the Sound of Islay, the channel separating Jura from Islay – the isle of many renowned distilleries. We appreciated the changing aspects and scale of Jura's mountains and the dramatic approach to the Sound, marked by the solitary white finger of the lighthouse at McArthur's Head. Strong tides run through the Sound; our arrival caught the beginning of the north-flowing stream.

Mid-way, at the narrowest part of the Sound, of a sudden on the Islay shore the compact settlement and ferry terminal of Port Askaig came into view; a link to both the mainland and a further local route to Jura itself. An RNLI lifeboat at its mooring added a flash of concentrated colour to the scene. The grandeur of the scenery on both sides was thrilling, enhanced by the quiet progress of the yacht, which was clearly demonstrating her prowess as a capable and robust floating home. We all took our turns at sail trimming and helming. The rig was so well 'balanced' that only touches of the helm were needed.

Not long after Port Askaig, two further surprises revealed themselves in succession from behind obscuring headlands: hard by the Islay shore the distilleries of Caol Ila and Bunnahabhain; whitewashed and bearing their names proudly in huge black lettering.

Our overnight anchorage was to be in a spectacular location; the approach requiring local knowledge and competent navigation: Loch Tarbert – a lengthy narrowing inlet which, as its name reveals, almost slices through the width of Jura. Edging slowly under power into an inshore basin protected by drying skerries, the anchor was streamed. Astern, the bulk of Jura loomed stark and forbidding, the internationally recognized geological feature of raised beaches, learned and quoted in exams for A-level geography, lay close to hand.

Thus far, the weather had shown its benign face but as it was also the period of autumnal gales, the dependable recited tones of the Shipping Forecast indicated that the following day would be one where prudence should be exercised. Launching the tender, a second anchor, bent onto a stout rope, was streamed in support of the main anchor. Throughout the ensuing inclemency a sharp eye was kept on events in case those anchors began to drag: they remained fast.

Showers and sunshine; entering the Sound of Mull from the west, approaching Rubha nan Gall lighthouse, near Tobermory.

Quitting our sanctuary, once more in favourable sailing conditions, *Corryvreckan* continued her passage northwards to round the northern extremity of Colonsay, beyond which, on the horizon, lay the lengthy bulk of the Ross of Mull. Lurking off its extremity an expanse of notorious sea-washed skerries – the Torran Rocks – provided an interesting inshore passage into the Sound of Iona.

Here we began our clockwise explorations of the Isle of Mull and sightings of many of her notable neighbours. Iona exuded its religious fame as meekly and effectively as the ruins of Lindisfarne, off England's northeast coast. Later, we closed with Staffa – and lingered in sight of Fingal's Cave, with its uncanny curtains of basalt columns. Towards the west our attention was drawn to an unusual and distinctively shaped island. One of the uninhabited Treshnish Isles, it was popularly known as Dutchman's Cap; its broad low expanse with central dome of rock indeed mimicked that particular style of headgear. For background, the two Inner Hebridean islands of Tiree and Coll formed a barrier to the Atlantic, creating a broad sea channel known as the Passage of Tiree. It afforded us a comfortable sail, now with the distant form of Skye as our forward prospect. Closer, the western extremity of the Ardnamurchan Peninsula, with its famous lighthouse marking the westernmost point of the mainland, became yet another moment to savour.

Following the trend of the coast we gradually entered the great waterway of the Sound of Mull. Rainbowed squalls guarded the entrance and provided an exhilarating approach towards our night's destination, Tobermory Bay.

The bay and the adjacent town of Tobermory kept their secrets until the last moment. A stocky lighthouse at the end of a raised walkway – Rubha nan Gall – slipped by and the indent of the sheltered bay slowly materialized. Craft at moorings appeared, a ferry terminal and then a waterfront promenade backed by brightly coloured buildings. To one of these we repaired during the evening: the Mishnish Hotel. Our skipper intimated that this was a place of pilgrimage for devotees of a true taste of Scotland. In the cosy back bar, with its subdued lighting, live Scottish music was being played by the hotel's owner, the acclaimed accordionist Bobby McLeod. Getting a round in at the bar, I found myself rubbing shoulders with an admired actor of stage and screen, Iain Cuthbertson, who latterly had played the lead role in the TV series *Sutherland's Law*. His imposing stature and soft Scottish lilt was all the more

CORRYVRECKAN SPINS YARNS

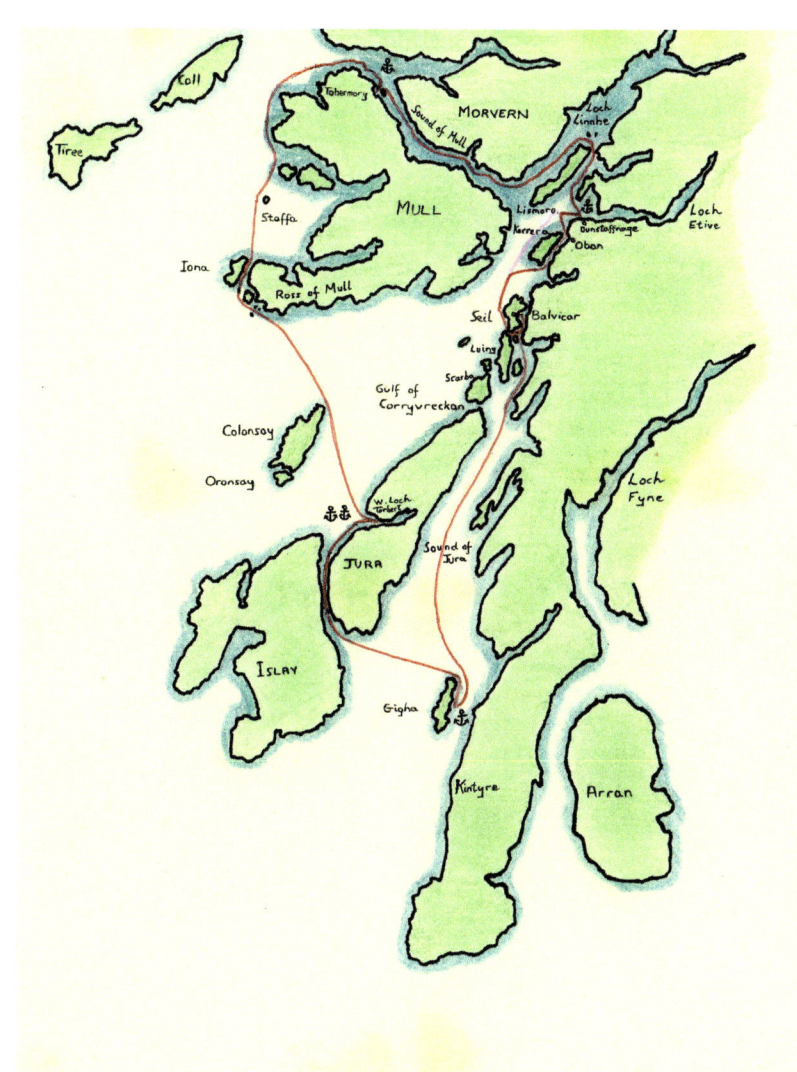

CRUISE OF "CORRYVRECKAN" 22-28 SEPT 1979

DAY 1 Joined 'Corryvreckan' at Balvicar, Isle of Seil

DAY 2 Left Balvicar, south down Seil Sound, east of Shuna Island, down Sound of Jura, to the Sound of Gigha and Ardminish Bay. ⚓ Ardminish Bay.

DAY 3 North up Sound of Gigha, west across Sound of Jura, through Sound of Islay, to W. Loch Tarbert, Jura. ⚓ N. of Beinn Bhreac, West Loch Tarbert, Jura.

DAY 4 Adverse weather, remained at Loch Tarbert ⚓

DAY 5 NW to N. Colonsay; to Ross of Mull; Sound of Iona, W. of Staffa, through Passage of Tiree to N. Mull. ⚓ Tobermory Bay, Sound of Mull.

DAY 6 Down Sound of Mull, up Loch Linnhe, to N. Lismore Island, down Lynn of Lorn southwards to Dunstaffnage. ⚓ Dunstaffnage Bay

DAY 7 To Oban Bay; Sound of Kerrera, and Sound of Insh, through the Cuan Sound into Seil Sound and Balvicar. Left the 'Corryvreckan'.

Corryvreckan's route for the week.

potent for his unexpected presence. He was a regular in Scottish coastal waters, taking time out in his motor-sailer *Sea Laughter*.

The onward passage eastwards through the Sound of Mull, flanked by the island and the bulk of the Morvern shore, led us to the Grey Rocks, a group of islets and shoals marking the transition into the entrance of Loch Linnhe. This great sea loch cuts northwards to distant Fort William, under the shadow of Ben Nevis.

Corryvreckan headed part way up Lower Loch Linnhe to round the northern tip of the island of Lismore, into the narrows at Port Appin. The more intimate surroundings of the Lynn of Lorn led us to the quiet seclusion of Dunstaffnage Bay, on the mainland, a few miles to the north of Oban. A stubby wooded headland concealed the compact yet impressive castle of Dunstaffnage, next to the laboratories of the Scottish Marine Biological Association with whom I would soon be associated, as an officer aboard their principal research ship, RRS *Challenger*.

Our final day of the cruise took us into Oban Bay, a mini-metropolis, transport-hub to the islands and centre for fishing boats and yachts. It was a scene of much activity; a contrast to the quietude of the rest of our voyage. The bustle of the bay retreated as we sailed sedately down the buoyed confines of the Sound of Kerrera, emerging into the Firth of Lorne and the Sound of Insh, passing the former slate-mining isle of Easedale. The narrow defile of Cuan Sound led us back into Seil Sound and to *Corryvreckan*'s home mooring at Balvicar.

My companion and I re-crossed the 'Bridge over the Atlantic' on our way home: the richer for having chosen *Corryvreckan* for our adventure.

*

Inspired by the participatory cruise aboard *Corryvreckan*, the following year, armed with information about the Corryvreckan whirlpool gleaned from the appropriate Admiralty Pilot Book, I ventured to Jura and trekked to its northern outlook across the Gulf where, over a period of several hours, I immersed myself in the reality of this extraordinary place.

AT CORRYVRECKAN

By Scarba and Jura, to the Gulf within,
Your meandering whirlpool, a dervishing temptress, spins
Dizzy notions. Across a decade I dreamed.
Corryvreckan you are deemed.
Upon what infamy are you blamed?
-That unseen, your nature is named.

To your bounded shores I ventured long.
Pulled by my fears and your siren-song.
At the turn of the tide brought greeting,
At decade's end came the meeting.
Low in your ebb, benign in humour,
Keenly alert, I kept watch for rumour.

As of wind in trees rose the roar,
To the heathered heights above Carraig Mhor.
Vantage of the vortex, arena of the westward scend,
Relentless against the scuff of wind, its surface trend.
Wedded in uneasy union, their offspring made mischief
In races, their respites brief.

Transformed by upwelling tears of deceit,
Smooth, like lily-pads on a ruffled pond, they became replete.
The cauldron simmered across its plain,
Above Scarba the mists condensed to rain.
In the excesses below, only sea-birds chanced;
Cormorant, gannet, and the nimble gull danced.

BOATS YET SAILING

The noisy mind stilled at the sight.
The disquiet of dreams was set to right.
Gone was fear; reality dispelled false ground
As the ghosts were laid in that watery sound.
Armed by quiet step, from whence I came,
'gainst future turmoil, as yet without name.

First broadcast: BBC World Service Merchant Navy Programme

Copyright: T.J.Boult 1980

CHILAWEE AND *CHIKANEE:* BIG SMALL AND LITTLE SMALL

Fruitful ideas can often spring unlooked for from the pages of books. Thus it was from Suzanne Beedell's *Country Living by Sea and Estuary*: a comprehensive manual for all who live (or contemplate living) by estuaries or on the coast. Having recently passed the official age-milestone into adulthood, and with two years of salary savings set aside as an indentured officer cadet in the Merchant Navy, the subject matter of the book proved compelling: the chapter on Small Boats especially so.

Under the sub-heading of *Acquiring a Small Fishing or Day Sailing Boat*, a particular full-page black-and-white photograph of the latter caught my full attention. Inspired, I leapt to the caption: *Cornish Coble: the standing lug has one set of reef points and the mainsheet is on a horse (bar) so that it can travel across the boat when it changes tacks; the bowsprit carries a useful foresail.* A product of the specialist builders, Cornish Crabbers, the image depicted a capable and seaworthy boat of undoubted character, forging close-hauled in open waters, with a backdrop of larger traditional-looking sailing craft by the same firm. In addition, the design was a modern interpretation of the cobles which I had come to know and admire at home. With the speed of thought, my mind was made up!

Youthful enthusiasm, when suitably motivated, can act with surprising speed and efficiency. In the late 1970s, communications remained traditional yet, before long, I was travelling alone by train to the furthest reaches of the Cornish Peninsula, to the home yard of Cornish Crabbers, at Rock, opposite Padstow on the Camel Estuary, for a test sail prior to making a potential order.

Taking up temporary residence near a public house on the quayside of Padstow, I entered into the spirit of the place by sampling a glass of scrumpy. Only when I hit the fresh night air on exiting did the effect hit me, as I briefly contemplated taking a shortcut across the corner of the quay. Getting to Rock the next day was also something of an adventure; a small local ferry operating across the estuary. The state of the tide required boarding by plank at the sandy waterside. It was a fine summer day and a satisfying breeze bode well for my forthcoming trial sail, which, yet again, did not disappoint.

A 'good thrash' was had and the boat handled responsively on every point: a very satisfying experience! Arrangements were duly made for an order, with one modification: the colour of the fibreglass hull. A deep bottle green was the standard for that hue, but I successfully petitioned for a different one; a paler and warmer green which may have rendered sail number 119 as the only Cornish Coble to have been thus liveried.

As the order was to take some months to complete, in the meantime I considered the matter of stowage and launching. A few miles up the coast from Cullercoats is the Port of Blyth, with its river of the same name. Campbell's Boatyard provided storage facilities and the port was in the process of laying official mooring trots in one of the river reaches nearby. The impetuosity of youth then decided that a small tender would enable the boat to be kept afloat at one of these new moorings. Familiar with the stitch-and-glue construction of the Mirror dinghy, I chose to build a kit tender from the design stable of Jack Holt. Still living at the family home during periods of short leave from my otherwise seagoing life as a cadet, the kit was eventually built entirely in my bedroom – as you do!

It was the same youthful enthusiasm that led me to making this seemingly sensible decision; my parents evidently attuned to the signs of probable eccentricity. The majority of the floor space had already been cleared of furniture years ago, to accommodate a long-standing model railway, which my brother and I had created in our teenage years. In one corner a large wooden chest of drawers provided a worktop and securing point for a small vice.

The hull of our Mirror dinghy was constructed by the 'stitch-and-glue' method, so I was familiar, in name at least, with the same method for the tender. I decided from the outset that I would try and build the craft to 'yacht standards', devoting as much time as was needed for that desired result. The process proved to be a fascinating mini-voyage of discovery, not only at realizing the various techniques involved but that I was actually capable of it: at school the woodwork teacher had been more than dismissive, giving his time exclusively to those with early talent. I made myself thoroughly familiar with the contents of the 'how to' booklet.

Shapes when flat can appear unusual, but they are made to express curves in more than one direction when fitted to create the form of a hull. There was no evident indication which side represented the joins to be stitch-and-glued in order to make the angled chines. I cannot now remember how I made my choice, only that it caused me anxiety; a jolt to confidence and an early lesson never to make easy assumptions or take anything for granted when boatbuilding.

The fastening method was indeed simple and effective, repaying patience in carefully marking out and drilling the adjoining small holes through which the copper wires were passed from the outside. Working from the transom, these were then twisted tightly to hold the joint whilst fibreglass resin and tape were applied. After drying, the excess of the twisted wire was snipped off so that a similar layer of tape could be applied to the inner part of the joint. The bedroom window was often widely open to dissipate the strong smells of the resin: the bedroom door kept tightly shut to avoid complaints.

The process was completed with the closure of the crest-shaped gap at the bow, to create the form of a pram; one of a number of very satisfying moments. Fitting out beckoned: gunwales, shaped breasthooks and quarter knees, thwart stringers, thwarts and their knees; crutch supports and doubling piece for an outboard motor; each a minor triumph, until, suddenly, construction was complete!

Temporarily clearing the floor by lifting the boat onto its transom for storage against the back wall of the room, there was a full inch of clearance beneath the ceiling. It suddenly appeared to have grown, and gave rise to another nagging doubt. As an inflexible three-dimensional object, would there be manoeuvring room, not just to exit the bedroom, but to negotiate the turn of the stairs and the subsequent descent to the front door? I decided to play it cool and embarked on the 'yacht finish' of paint- and brightwork.

My then current ongoing interest in heading out of Cullercoats in the beautiful coble *Admiral*, to assist in lobster fishing, had decided me as to the colour scheme. Like the coble, externally the hull would be rich green; the interior, cream. The rest, including the face of the transom, would be varnished. I particularly liked the detail at the sides of the thwarts, where varnish met cream in a semicircular join. I replicated this using masks of pre-cut sticky plastic sheeting. As the eyes are the last feature traditionally to be painted on images of the Buddha, bringing it to life, so, too, I painted the boat's name in green on the transom as the finishing touch.

It was to another book, and a favourite inspirational author, that the names of the coble and her tender were revealed to me. *Sajo and Her Beaver People* is a much-loved children's novel by the Canadian backwoodsman and conservationist, Grey Owl. The two main animal characters are young beavers, called Chilawee and Chikanee. From the Ojibwe Indian tongue, they translate as Big Small, and Little Small: a concept which I found not only charming but appropriate, as it gave me the opportunity to tangibly import into my own life my enthusiasm for what Grey Owl had stood for.

During this same period I chose a Mercury four-horsepower outboard motor, which would suit both the tender, and as an effective but lightweight auxiliary for the coble. An empty drum was procured, which, when filled with fresh water, provided the means of flushing the motor clean after use.

BOATS YET SAILING

Built at home in a bedroom, the kit tender *Chikanee* is finally completed.

The moment could not be put off any longer. With helpers assembled, the tender was manoeuvred through the bedroom door and turned turtle over the upper banister and newel post at the turn of the stairs. The critical point had been reached. Much twisting and exclamations of 'mind the wallpaper – and my fingers', accomplished the passing of the narrows, with snugness akin to a cruise ship negotiating the Corinth Canal. The unspoken fallback position was not needed: the removal of the three-paned stained glass windows – sporting scenes of square riggers in full sail – at the turn of the stairs. Once again upright and taking temporary residence in the garage, with the Mirror dinghy secured immediately overhead, a chandler would have been proud of the stock.

The maiden voyage of *Chikanee* took place at Killingworth Lake, a convenient manmade expanse of water in a somewhat urban setting. On a chilly winter morning, with a seconded school friend as helper and deadweight ballast, the ensuing trial was a reassuring and satisfying success. The collection of the coble from the far reaches of the Cornish Peninsula now beckoned.

A winter journey of such magnitude and a rig of trailer with large daysailer was not a task for my long suffering 900cc VW Polo. A large Ford Saloon with tow-bar was hired for a weekend.

Accompanied by my mother, intent on making the expedition a holiday, we packed for the winter journey, which promised seasonal delights. The vehicle comfortably ate the miles from Tyneside to western Cornwall. First sight of the coble next morning, already secured on her trailer, was a proud moment. The hull colour set off her lines beautifully. Administration completed, the long-haul out of Rock by minor roads was accomplished, as I got the feel of towing the boat, which completely obscured the rear mirror. The climate progressively became more wintry, making regular pit-stops at motorway service stations necessary. The hirer of the car accepted the keys next day but expressed surprise that the mileometer had registered an increase of one-thousand miles. Explaining the expedition, he shrugged his shoulders and may well have reflected on the term 'unlimited mileage'!

Surrounded by other wintering boats at Campbell's Boatyard in Blyth, I set to, painting *Chilawee* at the bows, and securing a detachable Silva marine compass in position. The creation of an ordered system of mooring trots in the river nearby was to prove a lengthy process, so the boat was to be launched and recovered by trailer. The VW Polo proved up to the task, even hauling up steep ramps, as well as on the open road.

To the north of Blyth the lower reaches of the River Wansbeck provided a suitable rural venue for *Chilawee's* springtime maiden shakedown voyage. My long-suffering father accompanied me as crew. Rigged and slipped into the water, the moderate easterly wind off the North Sea was coursing straight up the long reach: helpful for the boat to lie quietly whilst alongside during embarkation. Some months had passed since my trial sail in Cornwall, but I felt confident as the jib on its

The author takes *Chikanee* on Killingworth lake, for her maiden voyage.

Chilawee on her long winter journey north from the far reaches of Cornwall to Tyneside. My mother co-opted as 'crew'.

bowsprit was backed in order to ease the bow off the side, the mainsail already close-hauled.

As the sails began to draw nicely I had anticipated both some movement upwind and for the boat to begin heeling: neither happened, as we careered headlong towards the opposite bank in a classic 'ferry-glide' motion. My omission then dawned on me. Used to a daggerboard with the Mirror dinghy, which was physically in the way until lowered, the coble had a traditional weighted centreplate, housed in its central casing, which was raised and lowered by means of a pivot. It therefore required an act of memory to deploy it: a final detail I had overlooked. Annoyed and somewhat embarrassed, glad that there were no spectators, when the plate was lowered fully, *Chilawee* did indeed respond beautifully. The expression on my father's face mellowed after the initial unexpected dash, and we settled down not only to enjoying the capabilities of the boat under every point of sailing, but to see the changing landscapes, which were new to use both: we reckoned we were parochial explorers!

After de-rigging the boat and reversing the trailer into the water to accept her, it was then that the VW Polo first proved her own mini-might, as she hauled the complete rig up the angled concrete slipway: another potential complication evaporated. The location became a favoured one, for sails with the wider family, until early summer when *Chilawee* was to be inaugurated in the waters of the North Sea, outward from North Shields. As crew, I had the two who had traditionally been helmsmen during the 'Mirror Years', my brother and his father-in-law, Joe. The lower Tyne estuary was our historic stamping ground, but sailing in an albeit modern interpretation of a famous type of local craft, the sailing cobles proper of the home coasts, made it all the more special. I had not seen another Cornish Coble in these waters and I hoped that she may have drawn some interested eyes, from the Fish Quay and the wider promenades and mighty entrance piers. Keeping clear of the main navigable channel, we did raise appreciative glances and hand-waving from passengers on the outbound DFDS liner *Winston Churchill*. Clearing the South Pier and into the open sea, *Chilawee* took the chops in her stride, as all three of us experimented at the helm. Eventually lowering sail and motoring back, the little outboard in its integral slot at the stern drove us with a lively speed.

My plans and dreams for *Chilawee* and *Chikanee* did not mature: like their beaver namesakes who grew up and moved on to build their own lodges, the need for me to obtain a mortgage to purchase my first home, in the far north of the county, necessitated their conversion into cash. *Chilawee* headed south down the M1 after a rendezvous with the purchaser at a motorway services; the proud new owner of *Chikanee* was a wide-eyed young boy whose delight and enthusiasm at the prospect could not be dulled by his parents during the pre-sale negotiations. Once more, the Mirror dinghy slung under the garage roof was alone, but would relocate to the wooden double garage at my home in the Borders.

It would be many years hence, but where *Chilawee* had first sailed on the Tyne, I would take the helm of a real – large and powerful – traditional sailing coble.

Chilawee outbound on the River Tyne from North Shields, for a coastal sail in classic coble waters.

BOATS YET SAILING

REMEMBERING BLIGH AND SHACKLETON

Historically, the humble ship's lifeboat has been involved in some of the most arduous and acclaimed voyages of necessity ever made by small craft.

When William Bligh commanded HMS *Bounty*, after the infamous mutiny of certain crew, he and eighteen loyalists were dispatched from the ship in her launch. The ensuing voyage to safety of some 4,000 miles in the Western Pacific was a remarkable feat of endurance and skill. Similarly celebrated is that of the *James Caird*, a lifeboat from the ill-fated *Endurance*, the expedition ship commanded by Ernest Shackleton, which was destroyed by Antarctic pack ice in the Weddell Sea. The 800-mile passage he made in the lifeboat from Elephant Island to South Georgia, with five companions, to secure rescue of the main body of the stranded members of the Imperial Trans-Antarctic Expedition, has been officially regarded as one of the greatest small boat journeys ever completed. They both owed much to the heavy canvas sails and simple spars which made up their rigs.

Many unsung voyages have also been made by similar craft from warships and merchantmen, in extremis; especially in wartime. Merchant ships ply the oceans of the world and carry lifeboats as an integral part of their lifesaving equipment. Modern lifeboats are no longer designed or equipped to make potential voyages. The priorities are to maximize capacity, safe and rapid deployment, provide shelter from the elements and a powered means of clearing a stricken vessel in order to gather with other boats or liferafts, in anticipation of rescue initiated by modern systems of communication.

Until relatively recent times, it was standard for a merchant ship to carry both motorized and basically un-powered lifeboats in combination. The latter were routinely equipped with a simple sailing rig. In the Merchant Navy it was a custom that the Third Officer, as part of extra non-watchkeeping duties, regularly inspected and initiated maintenance and repairs to all the life saving equipment. This was a role I partook in as a young officer. On the oceanographic research ships of the Natural Environment Research Council, over forty years ago I was attached to the RRS *Shackleton*, a tiny vessel which had, under her previous guise with the

British Antarctic Survey, made a record for penetrating further south into the Antarctic than any other. She carried a single lifeboat on each side, one of which relied principally on sails.

During a lengthy scientific study in the Red Sea, the opportunity was taken of the fine weather to carry out in-situ major maintenance to the motor boat, which had an aluminium hull. Wooden outriggers and safety nets protected the crew who stripped the hull back to bare metal, prior to priming and recoating. In the open boat opposite, the heavy canvas sails, necessarily tightly stowed in equally substantial canvas bags, were often subjected to the excesses of weather and spent much of their time damp. As both a training exercise at rigging

In hot climes, on the Royal Research Ship *Shackleton*: maintaining the aluminium hull of the starboard lifeboat…

the lug sail and jib, inspecting their condition and giving them a good airing, it was a novel sight and gentle reminder that this humble boat was of a pedigree that could still carry out a passage. Supplies of fresh water and emergency rations were already on board, and a hand-cranked radio transceiver could make both Morse and verbal communications on recognized emergency channels.

Across a span of many years I witnessed the general trend towards modified systems of evacuating personnel and passengers from merchant ships. As the magnetic compass remains a potent 'low-technology' piece of 'fail-safe' marine equipment, the knowledge of what can be achieved by a simple sail remains a comfort and an inspiration.

...and airing the sails on the port lifeboat.

BOATS YET SAILING: THE INTERNATIONAL BOATBUILDING TRAINING CENTRE

1985 marked the occasion of 'the seven-year-itch'. I had been a qualified and serving officer in the Merchant Navy since 1978. For various reasons the gilt was beginning to wear off the braid. The period also coincided with a down-turn in the specialist sector of shipping and attractive offers of voluntary redundancy were on the table.

At a mid-voyage port call at Falmouth, on a walk ashore, I felt drawn into the famous nautical bookshop in the high street. Absently scanning the tightly stocked shelves my eyes lit on a particular title. The book, *Boat Building Techniques Illustrated*, was a seminal work by Richard Birmingham. It was a fateful moment, as I digested the first paragraph of the introduction:

There is a fascination in the intricate shapes and curves of a boat under construction that is like the fascination of the sea itself. For those involved in the work, the pleasure of creating a boat's shape, giving it strength, and eventually finishing it with an attention to detail that will enhance the vessel's natural grace, is matched only by the satisfaction of a successful launch. The cumbersome object is transformed: the dead weight that was agonisingly awkward to move to the water nods and dances on it with astonishing ease, like a young animal taking the measure of its first moments in life …

At that point I did not turn the page, which may have been fortuitous, as the introduction continued:

Headaches, - that is what boatbuilding is really all about. The image of the boatbuilder as a craftsman, at one with nature, his work a therapy for the twentieth century, unfortunately just does not ring true. To enjoy boatbuilding one must be ready to take on an endless stream of problems, and solving them must be considered part of the fun …

I also noted that there was a specialist centre in Suffolk dedicated to training and qualifying students in the construction of wooden boats. In fact, many of the illustrations were taken of miscellaneous craft being built at this venue: the International Boatbuilding Training Centre – IBTC – at Oulton Broad near Lowestoft.

The next stage of my life was determined in an instant. At voyage-end, I secured a place at IBTC in the following year's full-time, year-long course, given three months' notice and applied for voluntary redundancy. A major change in lifestyle was necessary. My first home near Berwick was put on the market and the redundancy money paid for an old fisherman's dwelling on the waterfront of the charming East Neuk village of St. Monans, in Fife. Only yards away was the famous boatbuilding firm of James Miller, at that point still engaged in supporting the needs of the local fishing fleet based at nearby Pittenweem and respected as creators of the Inchcape motor-sailers.

Before making the transition, I was given a detailed tour by the manager of the equally well-known boatyard at Eyemouth, which served its own fishing fleet as well as contracts with the RNLI. Many of the stout wooden vessels were known to me since childhood, closely observed during regular holiday visits. I was prospecting well in advance and entertained notions of approaching Millers in due course. It was ironic that during my year-long absence, Millers sold the yard and their name to a West Coast concern which used the yard to assemble prefabricated steel structures brought in by lorry from elsewhere. If nothing else, whilst waiting for the course to begin, I had realized another ambition: to live in Scotland. In that time I had the satisfaction of renovating my humble home into a desirable dwelling, with the aid of a 75% grant and a subsequent extra injection of funds into the bank to sustain my changed circumstances.

Wintertime and the early spring in St. Monans were filled in part by projects aimed at priming myself into the world of woodworking: from a second-hand shop, an ancient pine wall cupboard turned grey with age and the grain raised to a rasping roughness was transformed back to a smooth, polished and honey-hued item which is treasured to this day; a night-class at the nearby senior school enabled the construction by lathe of a 'rock lighthouse' table lamp, made out of yellow jelutong and red meranti woods, which, together with a marine chart shade, eventually found interest in the pages of *Woodworker* magazine. The contents of *Wooden Boat* magazine were devoured regularly. At the Scottish Fisheries Museum in Anstruther, I was a regular volunteer in carrying out aspects of interior restoration work on a small open 'double-ender' fishing craft, peculiar to the eastern coasts of Scotland.

The springtime journey southwards to Suffolk commenced by removing the contents of

THE INTERNATIONAL BOATBUILDING TRAINING CENTRE

the property into long-term storage so that the comprehensive renovations could begin in my absence; and driving to Tyneside in a full-to-bursting VW Polo for a stopover at my parents. I had arranged accommodation in an amply sized traditional caravan at Knight's Creek, on the shores of Oulton Broad. It was to become a bachelor pad and an exclusive study; a temporary home which became just one facet of what was to be a fascinating and extraordinary year.

*

Taking up my solitary residence in the caravan on a late Saturday afternoon, there was the delicious prospect of exploring the locality, and Sunday to extend my wanderings further, before beginning the course. I wasted no time in taking to my bicycle to seek out the IBTC; off Harbour Road – a suitably nautical sounding location. I was conveniently placed, within easy walking distance, if need be. Along with my fellow students, I was to discover it would not do to be late: the Centre was run on 'factory' lines. It was to be the first time in my life that I had 'clocked in',

The author's temporary home at the caravan site at Knight's Creek, Oulton Broad.

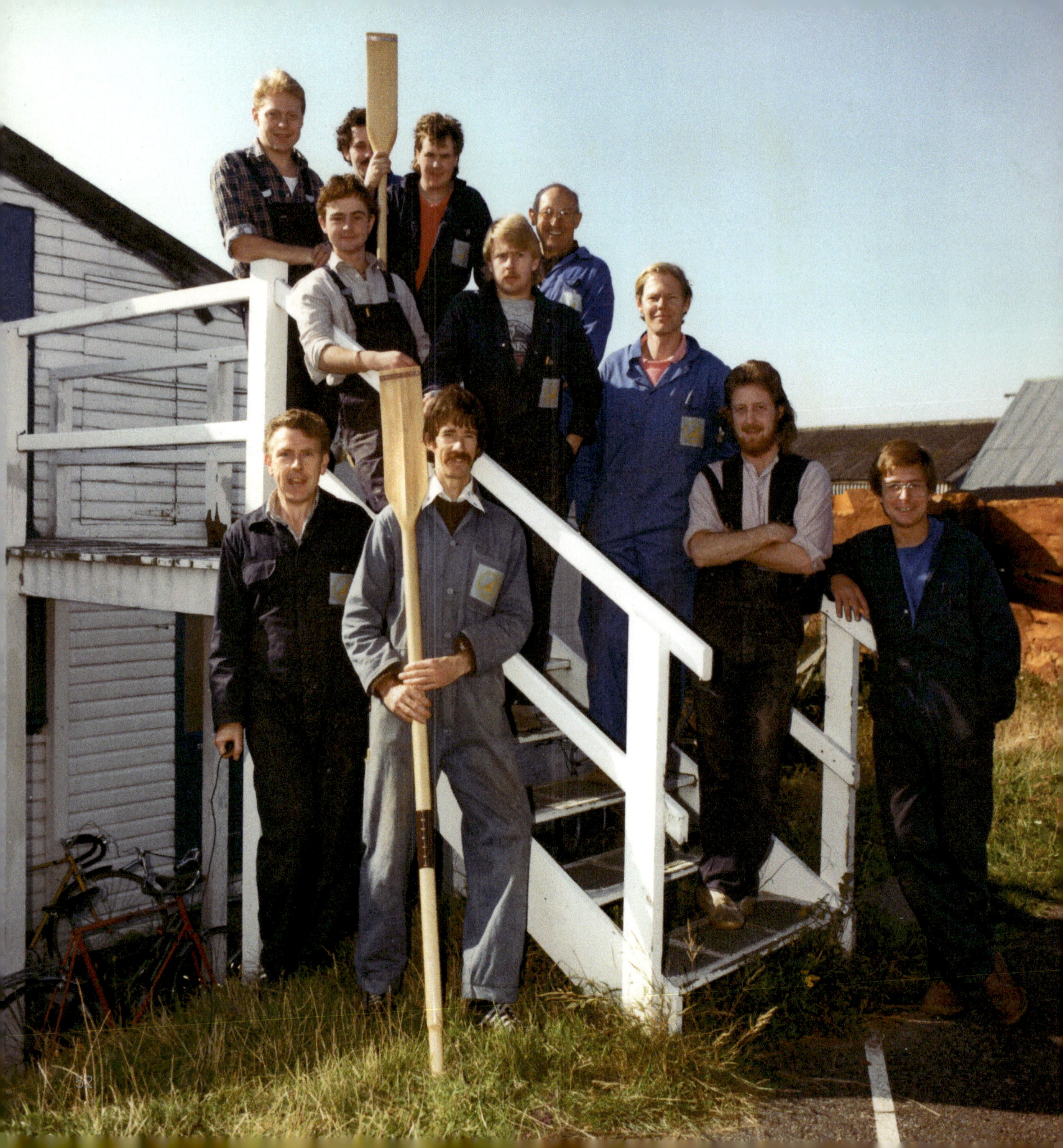

and attendance was closely monitored. It was all part of training students for the commercial workplace. Yet, as paying students, it was also bizarre to think that we were, in effect, the employers!

A corporate identity was expressed in the requirement to wear blue boiler suits, with a pocket badge displaying the Centre's logo. On the grounds of economy, I had cold dyed two white boiler suits from my previous employment before having the badge sown on. They turned out a pastel shade, which faded progressively with periodic washing. However, made to last, they continue in service to this day.

The process of initiation was similar to that at any educational establishment. There was an air of exclusivity, as the 'Class of 86-87' was comprised of eleven students. We were a mature, eclectic mix, in that there were representatives from several different countries, Australia and America included, and came from previous employments: a naval architect, a cabinet maker, retired freight airline pilot and a marketing executive.

The training ethos of the Centre was based on fulfilling orders made by clients who would obtain a finished craft, built under strict supervision and official Lloyds standards. Costs were essentially limited to materials: labour was free. The only proviso was that the construction time would be longer.

Issued beforehand with a preliminary tool list, we severally took up our positions at a full size woodwork bench. For the first term we would not go near a boat. Starting on a level playing field, regardless of previous knowledge, we were to be given an intensive graded training in carpentry and hand-tool skills. Also assessed to the highest standards – with work deemed defective publically consigned to the scrap box – the students had the growing satisfaction of making their own tools and pieces of equipment peculiar to boat building. Later, practice pieces allowed us to become confident in making more complex items.

Our initial task was to make a bench hook – to hold timber in the process of being cut by hand saw. Made from two pieces of mahogany, which had to be squared by plane and joined seamlessly, the screw fixings of the two hook pieces were hidden in counterbored holes covered by hardwood dowels. It was a sense of achievement and a relief to have this simple finished item measured and inspected closely, with a nod of approval from our joinery instructor: a good start!

It was a leap to then make a lidded oilstone box, beech wood mallet, a wood and brass spirit level, dovetail joint marking gauge, practice pieces with a range of mortise-and-tenons,

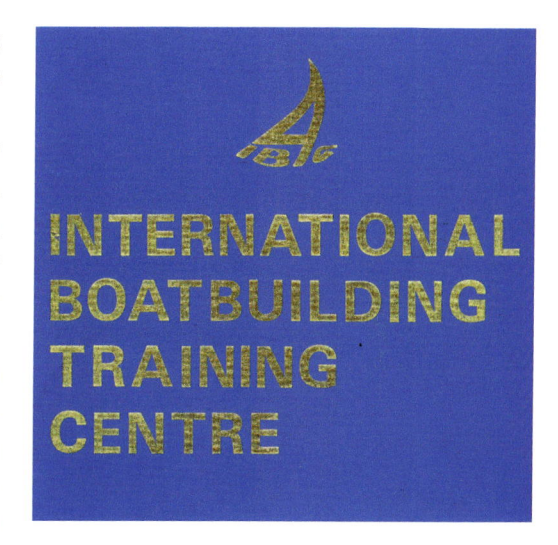

The beginning of an extraordinary year at the IBTC, at Oulton Broad, near Lowestoft, Suffolk.

Opposite: The year's intake: all mature students, they came from a variety of countries. By the railing, the author proudly displays his spoon oar.

Each student made a beech wood 'bollow plane' for shaping the concave aspects of the blade of a spoon oar.

dovetail joints, internal and external mitre corners, a spar gauge used to mark a square section of timber into an octagonal one, as part of creating, for instance, an oar. A tiny beech bollow plane, which fits into the palm of the hand, was destined eventually to create the graceful curving of the blade of a spoon oar.

Almost unnoticed, the emphasis on quality instilled a quiet pride and desire to work at our very best. There was mounting pleasure to be had in the acquisition of the hand-eye coordination and judgement, which are integral to the safe and effective use of hand tools. The biggest single item was a mahogany tool chest, fitted out with wooden trays, holders for chisels and saws, a brass lock and spliced rope handles. All was finished to yacht standard of construction and brightwork. To mimic the companionway of a yacht, and a traditional wooden grating, a mahogany set of step ladders provided an equally intensive learning experience and an item to keep and use for a lifetime. The foot-square pot stand was made as a grating. It comprised over seventy individual joints which had to fit perfectly and to millimetre accuracy. More than one was heard to clatter into the reject bin.

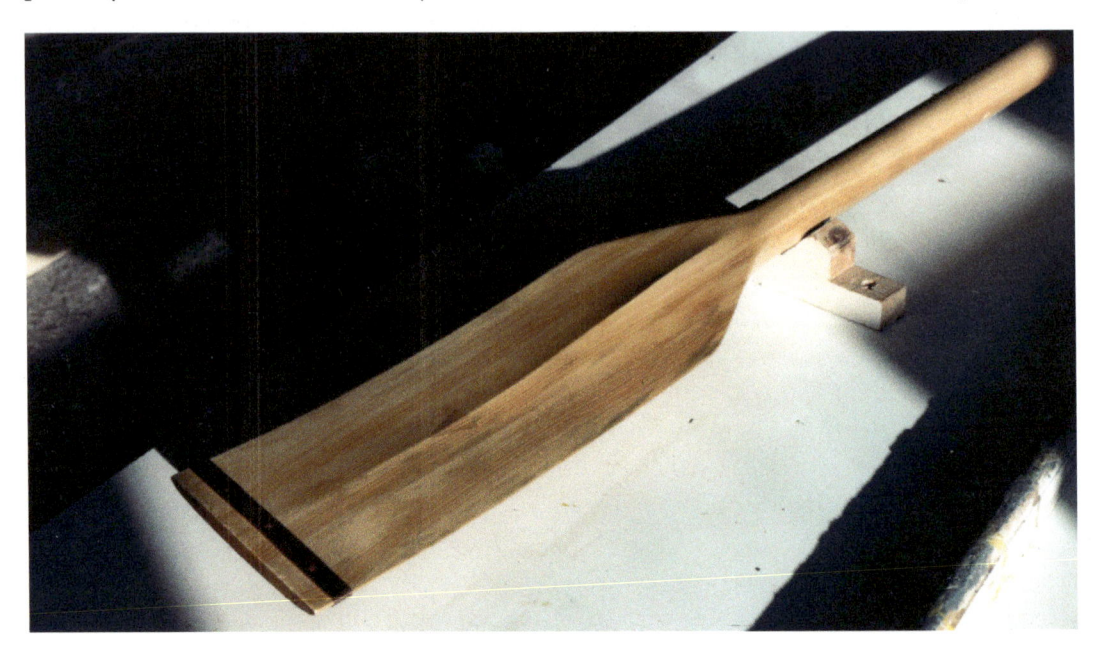

The author's completed spoon oar.

Throughout this period, regular theory sessions were held in a separate classroom, where the subjects of joinery and boat building were advanced in an academic manner. The conversion of both these sessions and indeed my own on-the-job notes kept me busy on most evenings. We were encouraged to seek out and acquire second hand tools. In nearby Lowestoft a wonderful old fashioned emporium provided an Aladdin's cave of such tools, and I did indeed acquire some excellent items to grace my toolbox.

It was the height of summer and some respite and recreation from the rigours of the course were sought. The city of Norwich could be reached by train from Oulton Broad and during an exploration I came across an RSPCA animal sanctuary in the western quarter. I offered my services as a Saturday volunteer, and was tasked to build, from scratch, a set of raised wooden hutches for rabbits and similar creatures. This proved to be a most interesting challenge, as was carrying my heavy tool bag across the city. Many of my recently honed skills came in very useful.

The local countryside was also suitable for cycling. As the whole area of the Broads is, by definition, one which is laced by fascinating stretches of rivers, cuts and wider reed fringed expanses, it was the perfect stamping ground to be immersed in observing the infinite variety of craft traversing these waters: and with an increasingly discerning eye for construction, form, function and grace. Within stepping distance of the caravan, Oulton Broad could be reached in pleasant minutes. There was nearly always some form of boating on the go, often from the local yacht club. Thursday evenings were given over to the annoyance of power boat racing, the volume of noise a major tedium to the conscientious student. I turned a negative into a positive and decreed that on Thursday evenings I would cycle inland to Somerleyton for a bar meal, thus enjoying both fresh air, pleasant exercise, and a meal and a jar put in front of me, with a fine rural vista across a curve of the River Waveney. An occasional local treat was had at the Wherry Hotel, with its own imposing waterfront panorama of Oulton Broad itself. Likewise, the nearby hostelry charmingly called

The author's completed tool chest and step ladders.

BOATS YET SAILING

Above and below: The RSPCA Animals Home in Norwich provided weekend voluntary work for the author, in scratch-building hutches.

THE INTERNATIONAL BOATBUILDING TRAINING CENTRE

Oulton Broad provided much visual inspiration for budding boatbuilders…

BOATS YET SAILING

Below: Northwards from Oulton Broad, Gorleston-on-Sea, on the River Yare, did similarly and with added glimpses of a former life as a navigating officer in the Merchant Navy.

The Lady of the Lake was a meeting place for fellow students, who referred to the venue as The Bitch in the Ditch.

Sundays also enabled visits along the coast, north to Gorleston on Sea, and south to Southwold. Each had their maritime interests and varieties of walks. Here, the local boats were again scrutinized, as a pleasant exercise and as fact-finding missions: how particular problems of construction or modification had been accomplished, which looked sea-kindly or cumbersome – and why.

The IBTC is located on the northern bank of Lake Lothing, a saltwater lake which issues into the North Sea and forms part of the Port of Lowestoft. It is connected to Oulton Broad by a lock. Lake Lothing was traditionally the major industrial centre with ship building and other engineering industries, much of which are now closed. In the mid-1980s there was still much activity on the banks, which were home to a disorganized cornucopia of craft: slipways for repair and maintenance of utility vessels such as tugs, berths for former trawlers that had seen a new life as oil rig standby vessels, any number and variety of leisure craft and, notably, an historic wherry drawn up on the stocks, her massive black clinker

58

hull standing proud above the workaday craft adjacent. An unofficial pathway through the area allowed for free access for the inquisitive.

The most senior student of our group was the retired freight airline pilot, William Muzala, from America. He had travelled to the UK with his wife and they fully embraced and evidently relished 'being English' for the duration: renting a rural cottage, buying a Morris Minor and two Raleigh bicycles for recreation. He also enjoyed the paternal accolade of being affectionately referred to as Ol' Bill.

Although being immersed in the world of boats, the lack of actually taking to the water for enjoyable recreation was a serious deficiency. Together with Malcolm, a fellow student and now long-term friend, we remedied this by becoming involved with the Oulton Broad Canadian Canoe Club. The organiser had a mini-bus and a trailer-full of these canoes. Sundays often found us and other keen members travelling about the region, enjoying the simple, quiet intimacy with the waterways through the maturing autumn and numbing but bright winter days. Becoming adept with the many subtle uses of the paddle, I invested in a beautiful six-foot 'Grey Owl' example: a work of art in its stripped construction and a joy to use.

The winter visit to Lowestoft by a

The picturesque coastal town of Southwold was a frequent location for Saturday visits.

Southwold offered many more opportunities to bask in the multifarious world of boats.

former marine scientist and friend, Vea Economides, was an opportunity to explain and demonstrate the workings of the IBTC and for a waterborne expedition in the canoe named *Log*. My involvement led me to being invited to travel to London to help man a stand at a national exhibition, promoting Canadian canoeing.

*

After the summer break, the 'Class of 86-87' returned to the IBTC with the exciting and slightly daunting reality of now being budding boat builders proper. In the main boat shed, a variety of craft were under construction, in varying degrees of completeness. The course was designed and run essentially to deliver, in one year, the comparison of two years of a four-year advanced apprenticeship at a commercial yard. To achieve this, individual students were assigned a wide variety of tasks across the range of craft being built, to maximize experience.

As we collectively entered the hallowed premises, with its scents of worked timber and oiled machinery, we were shown round by our instructor. Clinker hulled craft in preliminary and advanced states; a substantial carvel hulled yacht with as yet gaping spaces for planks, a motorized boarding boat for the RNLI, gleaming in dark blue topcoat, a capable-looking cabin launch in the process of being caulked and an upturned jig of a pram dinghy with the beginnings of cold-mould construction. We would certainly have plenty to get to grips with.

Two-dimensional theory was about to be translated into three-dimensional fact. Joinery is often about the junction of flat and regular surfaces: boat building is principally the creation of complex compound curved shapes, the meeting of which requires precise and rolling bevels in order to create a 'fair' hull form. Subsequent fitting out is then a combination of these two disciplines and, where appropriate, the application of rigging, electrics, plumbing and mechanical engineering. The two main methods employed for the creation of hulls were the traditional clinker and carvel: occasionally smaller craft were made from the strip method of using diagonal layers of veneer.

As our instructor Richard Birmingham explained: ... *On a clinker hull the planks overlap each other, the very visible run of the planking being a distinguishing feature. This ancient type*

BOATS YET SAILING

of construction produces a strong hull which is lighter than a carvel planked hull of the same strength and size. The lapped planks add strength, allowing both the omission of internal stringers and the use of thinner planking material than would be necessary on a similar size of carvel built boat.

Three very different clinker hulled boats were in the early stages of construction, allowing for a wider range of dealing with the practicalities of each. Eventually destined for HMS *Warrior,* Britain's first iron-hulled armoured battleship, on permanent display at Portsmouth Historic Dockyard, one of a pair of replica rowing gigs of considerable length

Lake Lothing, where the training centre is located, also provided much visual inspiration for budding boatbuilders.

62

required long runs of planking. These had to be joined by scarf joints but which were otherwise of a gently curving nature. The second boat was tiny: a daggerboard sailing dinghy, which comprised short but tightly curved planks and interior fittings. This proved to be a concentrated subject of techniques. The third was a pulling boat of intermediate size.

We had already benefited from the advanced training of the previous set of students nearing completion of their own course, part of which included the as yet mystical art of 'lofting' – the creation of a full sized two-dimensional representation of the form of the hull, in a set of three drawings collectively known as the Lines Plan. The body plan is used to obtain the boat's shape, where full size moulds are created, which, when spaced and held accurately, create a jig around which the hull is built.

The rowing gig had reached this stage, where the moulds had been set up at specific station intervals, and temporarily attached to the structure known as the backbone. This comprises the keel, stem and sternpost, and any other specific reinforcing members. These, too, will have

From America, Bill Muzala – O'l Bill – was a retired freight airline pilot.

BOATS YET SAILING

Sunday relaxation took the form of Canadian canoeing with a local club, paddling with Malcolm Lewis, a fellow student.

A visit from a former colleague and marine scientist, Vea Economides, was enhanced by an outing in 'The Log'

Local boats were scrutinized and assessed with budding boatbuilders' eyes.

THE INTERNATIONAL BOATBUILDING TRAINING CENTRE

Promoting Canadian canoeing at a London exhibition.

been the subject of critical building practices, given their intrinsic importance to the hull's structure and strength.

The clinker construction was described as 'larch on oak' – the planking of the coniferous larch, later reinforced by lengths of oak timbers steamed into place, the whole 'clenched' by cold riveting with copper nails and roves.

To the side of the boatshop, many carefully erected tiers of sawn larch boards, separated by battens, were being seasoned. These became the basic ingredient for transforming into a plank. To the inexperienced eye, after having completed various 'labours', the prepared plank still lying flat on the floor could seem a most unlikely shape. Yet, when offered into position to lie naturally against the moulds, it magically assumed the form of the hull, which grew from the keel upwards, on both sides. The careful planing of bevels and cutting of special rebates, known as geralds, allowed each plank to nestle and merge with its predecessor, to produce a run of lines which can make a clinker hull appear so attractive. The planks are held together by copper fastenings, the technique of clenching being an ancient skill, requiring particular tools with satisfying names: dolly, rove punch, ball peen hammer.

When the shell of the hull has been completed, the moulds and their supports are removed and a sealing coat of paint or varnish applied. Another satisfying and almost mystical practice – that of steam bending and locating the oak timbers – begins with the creation of a steam box and some form of boiler to generate steam. It has been observed that the combination of crude plumbing, makeshift boilers, and seeping steam ensures that every steam machine appears to have been designed by Heath Robinson. The freshly sawn oak timbers, which can be soaked for several days in advance, are placed into the steam box. After a prescribed time, the steam renders the timbers pliable – for a short period.

If possible a boat is timbered out in one prolonged session, which requires preparation and a well-organized team. The location of each timber is pre-marked, fastening holes pre-drilled and the copper nails inserted ready to be driven through the hot timber. Techniques vary, but essentially, each over-length timber is offered into position and gently bent and twisted to conform to the interior shape, then fixed with the nails. The completion of timbering out proved to be a satisfying achievement, for all concerned. Ahead, there still lay the time-consuming and tedious clenching of a myriad nails!

Thereafter, the fitting out of the hull required the making and shaping of many individual components, each with time-honoured names: bottom boards, gratings, stringers, thwarts, knees, gunwale, breasthook, rubbing strake. They also required considerations and quirky wrinkles of methods peculiar to the craft of boatbuilding. Construction complete,

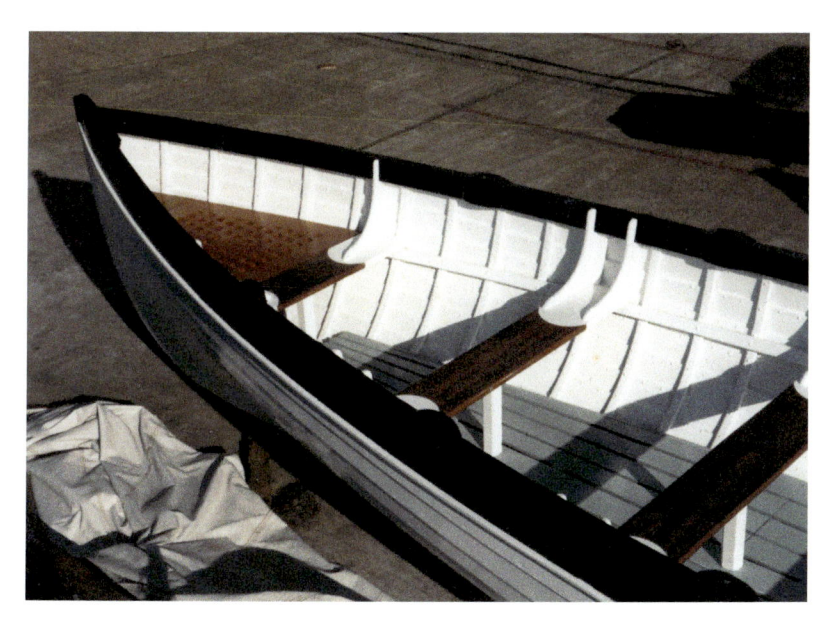

THE INTERNATIONAL BOATBUILDING TRAINING CENTRE

One of the rowing gigs destined for HMS *Warrior* begins to take shape.

BOATS YET SAILING

One of the completed gigs seen many years later in situ aboard HMS *Warrior*.

Construction of a clinker hulled boarding boat for the RNLI.

BOATS YET SAILING

Details showing construction of a clinker hulled boarding boat for the RNLI.

the application of paintwork and varnish is a fitting culmination; and as much a skill in its own right.

Special one-off items for a particular boat give tremendous scope for individual construction, such as ladder companionways, skylights, masts and spars, ballast keels. It was the luck of the draw for students to find themselves engaged in one or other of these components. One of the larger carvel hulled boats under construction was a long-keeled Bermudan sloop. This required a heavy lead ballast keel to be incorporated in the design. The ballast keel itself is cast at a foundry, using a carefully fashioned wooden 'plug' as a pattern. The plug is made at the boatbuilders and must also include precise locations for the holes for

The tight lines, curves and compactness of a small sailing dinghy proved an excellent training project.

the keel bolts. The 'Class of 86-87' was given a rare day out, as we piled into a mini-bus for a drive inland to the foundry, in order that we could view the casting process. For the student who had laboured long in creating the plug, it was a particularly memorable occasion: and a fascinating one for all of us.

The tiny clinker sailing dinghy enabled me to construct the lifting rudder and tiller assembly; and topcoat varnish the entire craft: a good way of reinforcing the 'naming of parts'! Classroom sessions continued, as the academic element was addressed and periodically assessed by formal multiple-choice questionnaires.

As the year was maturing and the night-time temperatures in the waterside environs of my caravan plummeted, I relocated to an adjacent brick chalet for the remainder of the course. It was still an experience akin to Captain Scott's cabin in the Antarctic, but with less effective heating! I had calculated to the nearest minute when I could emerge from beneath the bedclothes to breakfast on porridge and prepare my packed lunch, discovering a short cut through byway lanes to cycle to the waterfront of the IBTC.

*

The carvel hulled yacht under construction, using durable iroko hardwood planking, was of a more substantial order. Looming over our heads, planking from both the keel and from the sheer line downwards had already begun. Carvel planking produces a smooth hull, each run of planks butting against the next. The seams are rendered watertight with caulking cotton and stopping compound, or thin timber splines. Initial construction also uses pre-shaped moulds, set up in their respective places and firmly secured. To these a series of timber strips, known as ribbands, are temporarily nailed, creating an open basket form of the hull. Steam bent timbers are then offered into place and secured temporarily to the ribbands. In heavier constructions, timbers are fashioned cold, out of 'grown timber', a complicated procedure which creates a very strong hull.

The topmost plank – the sheerstrake – is permanently fitted to the outside of the timbers with copper nails. Plank after plank is then added to each side, the ribbands being taken off as the process progresses. Planking from the keel can also go on at the same time. As with clinker, the final shape of a plank requires many additional labours to achieve the desired result.

After all the planking has been copper riveted to the timbers, the exterior is planed off and glass-papered prior to an appropriate priming application of paint or varnish. When required, caulking and stopping of the seams may then be carried out. Thereafter, the fitting out of the hull is similar to that of a clinker craft. However, our limited experience was

Winter quarters at chalets near Knight's Creek, Oulton Broad.

Right: Part of the by-way cycle route between 'home' and the training centre.
Below: A graceful carvel Bermudan sloop introduced students to the complexity and beauty of construction and laid teak decks.

BOATS YET SAILING

Further photographs illustrate the graceful carvel Bermudan sloop.

THE INTERNATIONAL BOATBUILDING TRAINING CENTRE

Above and left: Stages in the creation of a mast.

BOATS YET SAILING

with open boats; the yacht was to have a fully laid teak deck, with cabined accommodation, a well towards the stern and auxiliary propulsion. We were about to learn a lot more about incorporating structural integrity with both strength – and elegance.

On completion of the yacht, there was a palpable corporate sense of great achievement; to some a revelation of the complexity, skills and labours which went into the creation of this gleaming new thing of undoubted beauty. Given that boats at IBTC are necessarily constructed slowly, it was lucky that the 'Class of 86-87' were to see not only the completion of two significant builds, but their individual journeys away from the Centre. The yacht was ceremoniously launched off her cradle into the immediate waters of Lake Lothing,

Below and opposite:
A half-deck cabined motor launch

THE INTERNATIONAL BOATBUILDING TRAINING CENTRE

assuming a more diminutive stature as her deep keel submerged and she floated spectacularly at her design waterline. The other craft was well advanced in her own construction.

The carvel hulled half-decked motor launch provided our training in caulking and stopping the seams: another technique steeped in history and using esoteric tooling and materials. Based on the principle that when the caulking cotton fibres get wet they swell, preventing any further penetration of water through the hull. Tightening the seams, effective caulking actually strengthens the hull. A two-stage process,

Above: Cold mould construction of the hull of a small pram dinghy.

Above right: Taking the lines off an existing boat for the purposes of reproduction or for historic documentary interest.

it requires much care and patience, before the seams are finally rendered flush with a putty sealant.

The same launch was also scribed with her waterline: another process utilizing a satisfyingly ingenious and 'simple' method, requiring only that the boat is level athwartships and that the location of the waterline is known and marked at bow and stern. At these two points, long straight edges are set up horizontally. These effectively represent the level plane of the water. By careful use of a length of taut line progressively slid along the straight edges, where it touches the hull a mark is made. These individual marks are then joined by use of a thin batten, the line scribed into the hull as a permanent mark. Painting the completed boat resulted in a smart and capable workhorse of a launch. Finished to the requirements of the owner, she was craned out of the boatshop onto a flatbed lorry, to begin her own life afloat.

*

The more modern construction technique of cold moulding was explored with a jig of a small pram dinghy. Here, the hull is laminated from several layers of veneers. Each strip of veneer is offered up to its fitted neighbour and marked to achieve a snug fit, the excess being trimmed carefully with a block plane. Successive laminations are laid diagonally across the one beneath, for added strength.

A pre-existing example of one of these boats was set up in order to practice taking a series of precise measurements from which another boat of the same design could be constructed.

The resulting Table of Offsets can then be used to generate the full size Lines Plan which defines the form of the hull.

Whatever the construction method of a hull, there comes a time with motorized craft, that aspects of engineering come to the fore: mechanics, plumbing, electrics; considerations for fuel, exhaust and cooling systems for an inboard engine. Before all this, the critical location and orientation of the engine on stout wooden bearers and its connection through solid structure of an aligned stern tube to accept the propeller shaft.

Having obtained practical hands-on experience in the construction of various hull forms, with a working appreciation of generating complex three dimensional shapes, it was timely to be introduced to the geometry and art of lofting: firstly with scaled down exercises, to produce aspects of the Lines Plan for an actual boat. Our instructor, Jack, the most senior at the Centre, indicated that the lofting precision and tolerances for boat building were actually less stringent as compared with that of the WW2 'wooden wonder' aircraft, the de Havilland Mosquito, which he helped to build in his younger days.

We were privileged then to work on the creation of the full scale Lines Plan for a pair of historic gun pinnaces, which would eventually also grace the decks of HMS *Warrior* in Portsmouth. The plans were generated from blueprints, which offered less than complete

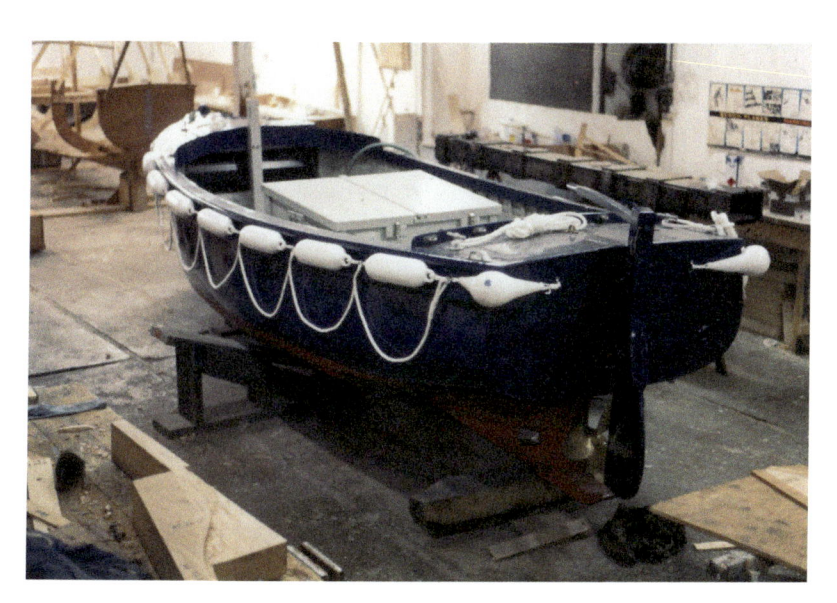

A carvel-hulled motorized boarding boat for the RNLI introduced students to many more skills of construction and fitting.

BOATS YET SAILING

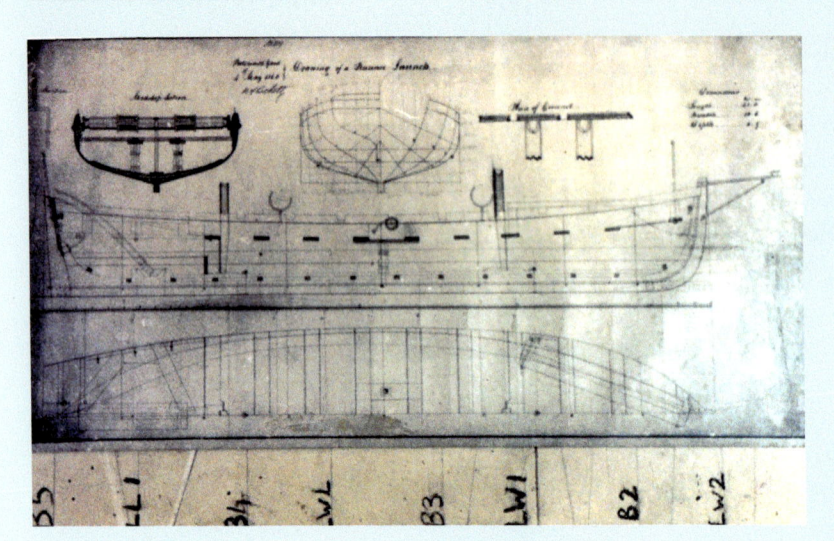

Historic plans for the heavy gun pinnaces of HMS *Warrior* were used for lofting training by students prior to construction.

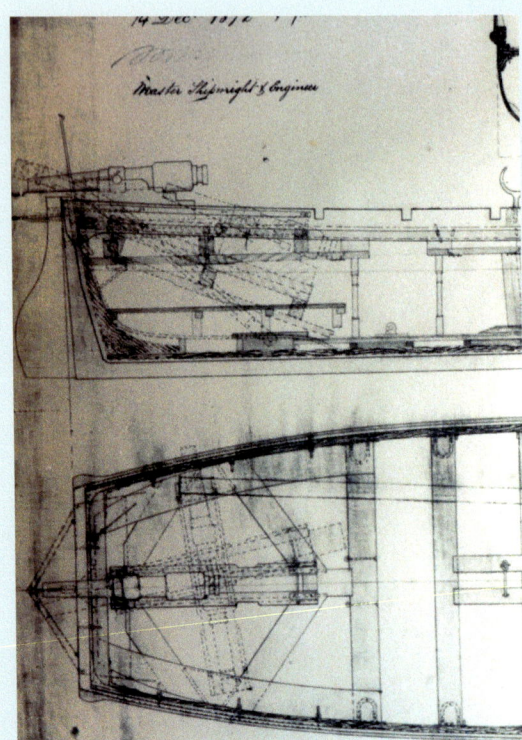

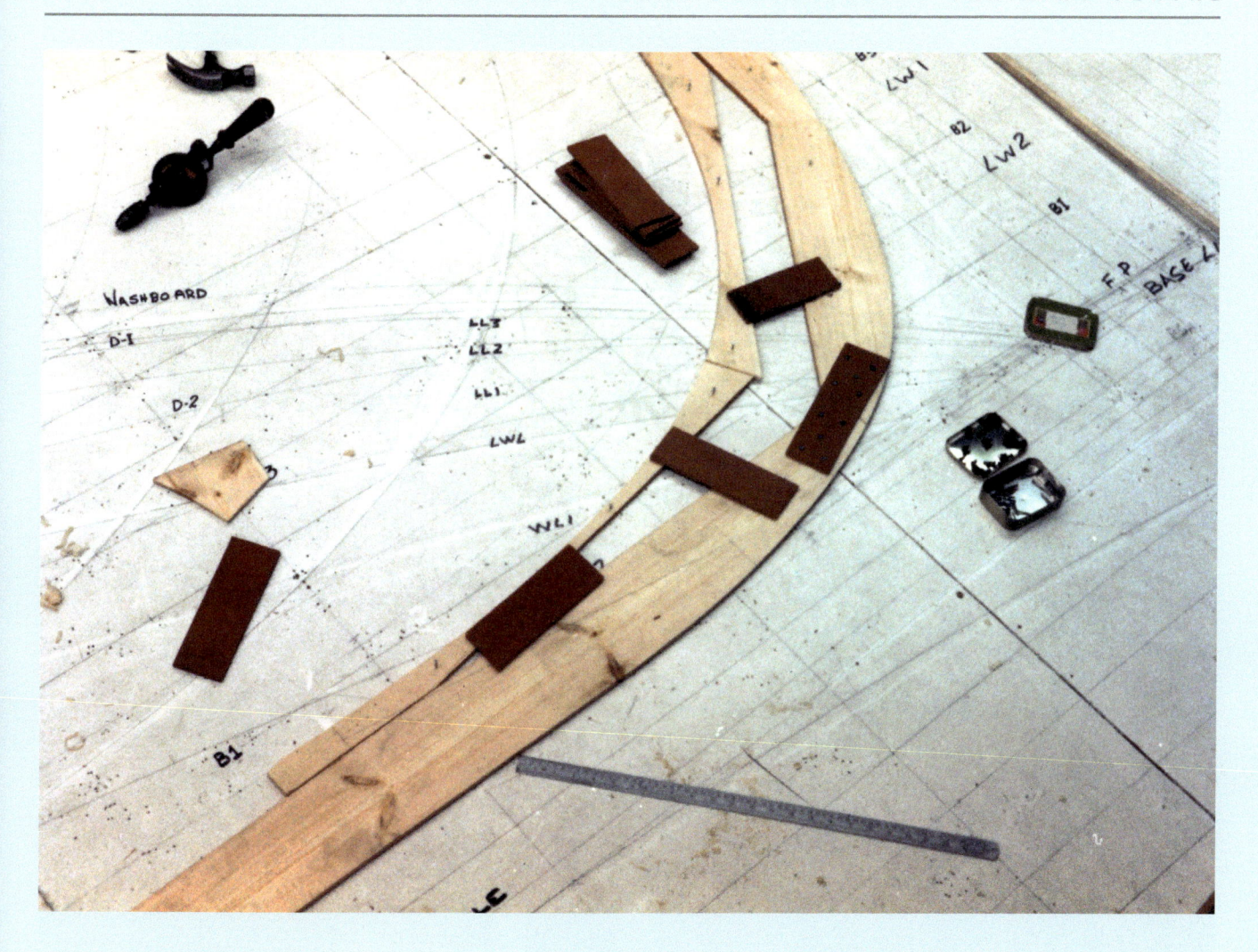

THE INTERNATIONAL BOATBUILDING TRAINING CENTRE

BOATS YET SAILING

The author later inspects one of the completed gun pinnaces on HMS *Warrior*.

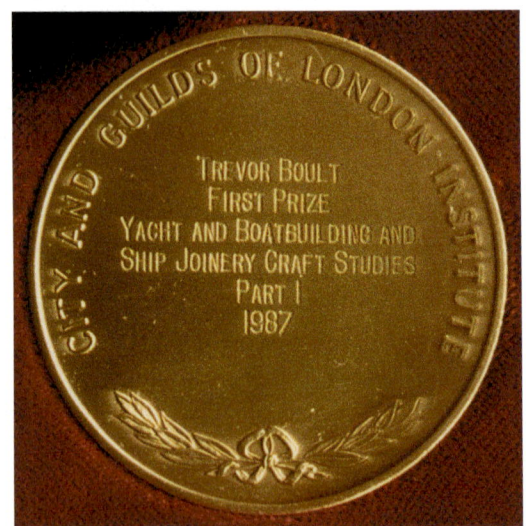

Time to leave for pastures new brandishing medal...

information: overcoming this was evidently an interesting challenge for our instructors.

From the completed full size plans, we were variously involved in creating the wooden station moulds and templates for the backbone structure. It was for the next set of students to be tasked to build these two historic craft.

Many years later, my wife and I visited HMS *Warrior*. It was another moment for quiet pride, touching the gleaming white high-gloss hull, with a knowing eye and to recollect one of the most significant and memorable of years; at the IBTC.

...and Diploma.

Boats Yet Sailing: a personal interpretation of an extraordinary year.

A RANGER AND SHEPHERD GO FORTH

The visit I had previously made to the Eyemouth Boatbuilding Company before commencing my training at the International Boatbuilding Training Centre had unwittingly created a latent connection, which I was to make some months later, whilst enjoying the environs of my new and modest home on the waterfront at St. Monans, that looks directly south across the Firth of Forth. The village's long association of building and repairing the fishing boats of Fife occasionally found unusual craft drawn up on the yard's cradle within the arc of picturesque colour-rendered dwellings that fronted the pier-protected inner bay.

My daily walk around the village to the open coastline beyond the well-known Fishermen's Church took me past this location. On the cradle was an interesting wooden vessel which had the hull form of a small stern trawler. However, the length of the deckhouse suggested a modified function. Experience from elsewhere made me conclude that I was looking at some kind of research vessel. On her transom, the name *Forth Ranger* introduced me to the boat which I would soon get to know in much more detail.

Built in 1976 at Eyemouth, *Forth Ranger* was the research vessel for the Forth River Purification Board, and based at Port Edgar on the southern shore close to the Forth Road Bridge. My usual curiosity led me to contacting the Board. This innocent enquiry unexpectedly opened the door for an invitation to sail on the *Ranger* in an official supernumerary capacity. With recent professional experience of working on research ships, and with a superior qualification necessary for the *Forth Ranger* to occasionally work beyond her usual seaward limits, I was given permission to occupy the boat overnight so as to be available for her early departure the next day. Gaining access late on in the evening, armed with sleeping bag, ablusions and suitable clothing, the night proved memorable. The muted excitement of a new venture in prospect was enlivened and disturbed by the incessant squealing of the heavy rubber fenders – akin to the cries of distressed seals – in response to a ground swell that penetrated the harbour.

Notwithstanding, the arrival of the crew, the bringing to life of the boat, our departure into the sun- sparkled Forth, the periodic sampling activities which punctuated the changing shore

BOATS YET SAILING

The Forth River Purification Board's research vessel *Forth Ranger* completes refit at the author's home: St. Monans, Fife.

vistas from upstream, and led eventually to the environs of Bass Rock, the massive gannet-laden guardian at the southern approaches to the Forth, was a pleasurable sortie back to sea.

Such was the clarity of the day that the coastal villages of the East Neuk of Fife could be made out. The new hi-rise pale grey 'shed' of the boatyard at St. Monans stood out incongruously. Under construction within its masking enclosure was another vessel which would accrue quiet renown over many years. Of steel construction, assembled from prefabricated units made elsewhere, *Good Shepherd IV* was to make the challenging waters between Shetland and Fair Isle her home. Her initial appearance from within the shed on the occasion of her launching was one of fluttering bunting and cheers from the assembled crowds on the pier. When fitting out was completed, the diminutive yet resolute-looking craft carried out trials locally before making passage eastwards out of the Forth to begin her life in northern waters.

I would soon be heading south, towards fresh territories of my own.

The launch of the Fair Isle supply vessel, *Good Shepherd IV* at St. Monans.

A PRICELESS CHIPPENDALE IN WROXHAM

The late Jack Chippendale is warmly acknowledged as one of the finest wooden boatbuilders of the recent past. Proud owners of classic sailing dinghies such as the clinker-hulled Merlin Rockets and National 12s, the high performance Fireballs and more recently the handy 'plastic' car-toppable Topper – originally called Chipmunk after his development of the original plug for the hull – have cause to celebrate his commitment to perfectionism. His beautifully crafted boats dominated dinghy sailing in the 1950s and '60s. In the 1970s, Jack Chippendale moved to Norfolk and later helped establish a boat building and repair facility at Wroxham Barns, in the heart of the Norfolk Broads.

*

Towards the completion of my course at the IBTC I was approached by one of our instructors, Richard Birmingham, who quietly relayed an extraordinary and unlooked-for offer of employment. Apprised of the facts, and excited at the prospect, I found myself one Saturday driving across Broadland to the important boating hub of Wroxham: my destination, Wroxham Barns – an arrangement of former farm buildings which had been converted to support a range of small craftwork businesses and which lay on the outskirts of town. My prospective employer was a key member of the group who oversaw the conversion of the complex – Jack Chippendale.

His establishment formed one arm of the facility; the largest single unit on site. I was met by a kindly-looking gentleman in work attire and faded canvas cap, reassuringly akin to the driver of a steam locomotive, who made me feel instantly at ease. This was the man himself and I was only to discover later the extent of his stature in the world of boatbuilding. Shown round the boatshop and then the rest of the complex, I was advised what my employment would entail. I was to be the sole employee and, in recognition of my trainee status, would be mentored and receive a commensurate and representative wage. A handshake introduced me into the exciting, and exacting, world of professional wooden boatbuilding.

Back at Oulton Broad I was able to thank Richard for brokering the opportunity in the first place: a boost to my confidence, which yet also cast its accompanying shadow of doubt, of actually 'being up to it'. I pressed on with resolving another matter: accommodation. Having become used to the more financially simple arrangement of living in a rented caravan or holiday chalet, I decided initially to secure something similar nearer to my new work place. A smaller caravan was chosen at a quiet little site at Potter Heigham, to the east of Wroxham. Potter Heigham is also a notable hub for the world of boating on the Broads. The banks of the river, and of course its famous low-arched bridge, were to become the focus of my evening walks.

The need for economy in this exciting yet uncertain time allowed me the opportunity generally to cycle the ten rural miles to and from Wroxham, having earlier deposited my tool chest at the boatshop. A new routine of shopping for groceries was established, as was the making of packed lunch, just as I had done whilst at the IBTC. The outward cycle – often against the prevailing wind – was more of a psychological and physical effort: the return journey, a more pleasant one, the memories of the day at the boatshop occupying my thoughts. I soon discovered that Jack's gentle mentoring, by talking through whatever task I was set, was

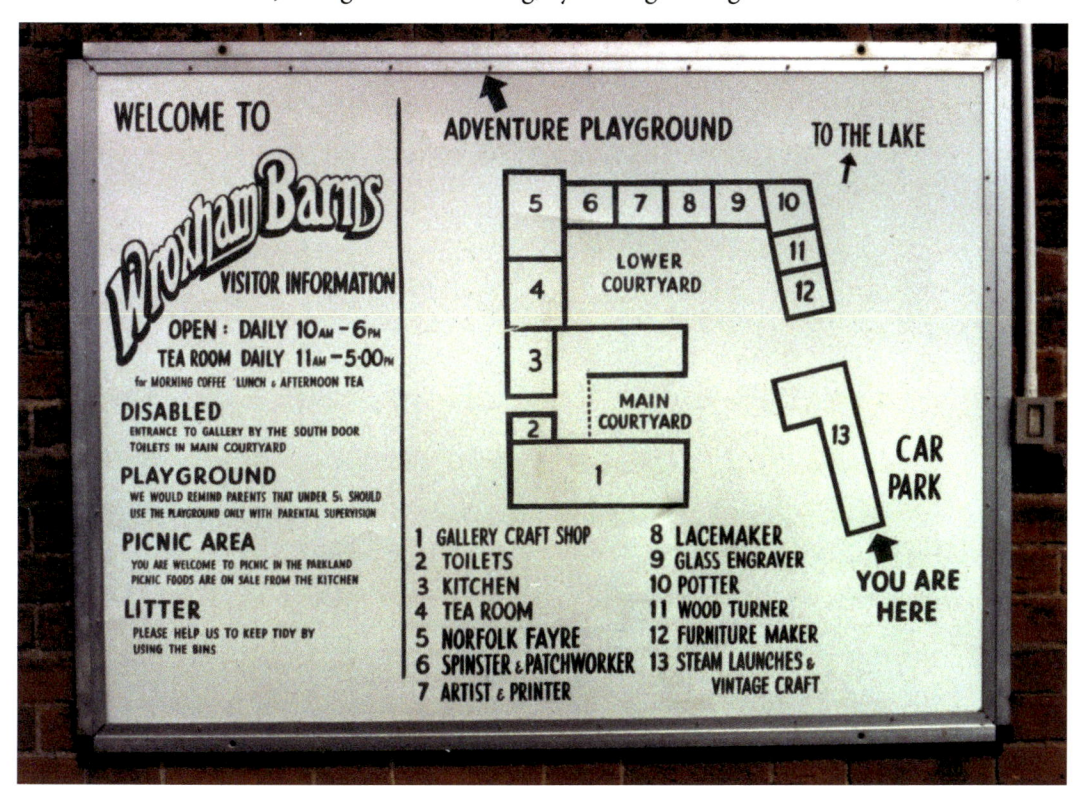

At the entrance to Wroxham Barns, lucky number 13 was the base for Jack Chippendale's vintage craft centre.

as precious as gold: I felt I should record every bit of advice; on techniques; materials, quirky tricks of the trade: I was privileged to be offered a lifetime of knowledge, presented in a low-key, conversational manner. I continued my established practice during evenings and at the weekend of translating my notes into a working journal.

At this time, work tended to focus on repairs to smaller wooden craft and the long slender hulls of rowing skulls from the region's rowing clubs. It was part of the working remit of the units at Wroxham Barns that the craft businesses be open for observation by prospective purchasers of goods, or as part of a visitor attraction. The idea of an educational element for the general public brings benefits, and pitfalls. The boatshop proved attractive, with its aura of tradition, multifarious scents and assortment of craft in differing stages of repair or renovation. Pausing midway through a task requiring precision in order to answer a question can make resumption a time of risk, the flow of concentration having been interrupted.

In 1983, Jack Chippendale had co-designed with Andrew Wolstenholme the 15ft Sprite rowing skiff, acknowledged as 'a fine rowing boat' and which was later copied in the USA, to

A range of small craft under construction or repair, including Jack Chippendale's co-designed kit rowing skiff.

be sold as the Merry Wherry – a name linking back to the Broads. The boat was marketed as a kit for home completion. It was an aspect of my job to create the parts.

Another occasional facet of the boating world was introduced to me here. Jack was an appointed Sail Measurer. Sailing craft, such as one-design racing yachts and dinghies, must comply with a strict code of measurements, whether of the hull or sails. Occasionally, a new suit of sails would appear for verification. Downing tools, each sail was carefully laid out on the smooth forecourt and the critical measurements recorded.

As time passed I gave some thought to changing my accommodation, my eyes lighting on a houseboat moored in Wroxham itself. The idea proved adventurous and superficially attractive, but also raised many practical and financial doubts. I knew nothing about living on a houseboat or the realities of maintaining them, or their value as an investment. Another factor caused me not to pursue the matter. A commitment made before I had been offered the job at Wroxham Barns was approaching. Jack understood and was supportive that such commitments should be honoured. My vacated position was to be filled by a YTS trainee, with the opportunity later in the year to return to Wroxham.

As I headed northwards, with the VW Polo once more laden to the gunwales, to take up residence at the Calvert Trust Adventure Centre for Disabled People, in the Lake District, as a voluntary sailing instructor throughout the summer months, I little knew that the experiences would, in turn, lead me off in more new and exciting directions.

*

In my principal profession in the Merchant Navy, having eventually attained my British Master's Foreign Going Certificate of Competency, I retain as much quiet pride – and sense of privilege – to have been for a short time not only a professional wooden boatbuilder but a trainee of Jack Chippendale, at his specialist centre at Wroxham Barns in Norfolk.

A job as a professional boatbuilder: the author's new residence at a caravan park at Potter Heigham.

BREEZES ON BASSENTHWAITE

Serendipity – the happy chance – can suddenly appear in the most unexpected places. In the mid-1980s, one such occurred for me on the slopes of a mountain in the Lake District.

Inspired since teenage-hood by the unique graphic writings of Alfred Wainwright – AW – in his pictorial guides to the Lakeland fells, and used reverentially across a span of many years, I eventually adopted one of AW's celebrated traits: that of the solitary and somewhat anti-social hillwalker, the better able to connect personally with the landscapes being explored.

Towards the end of one particular day, advanced in my descent from a notable horseshoe of fells, I observed another solitary walker converging from a different direction on another path, evidently intent on taking the same descent to the valley bottom. Meeting was inevitable, as was the courtesy of the hills, to at least make an acknowledgement. We found ourselves not only in step, but strangely inclined to converse. Before long, my pleasant companion related how, as a local, he helped out as a volunteer at the Calvert Trust Adventure Centre for Disabled People. Poised on a hillside overlooking Bassenthwaite Lake to the north of Keswick, it offered a wide range of outdoor activities geared up for groups of people with special needs. This included a comprehensive water activities facility, which utilized the nearby lake. Craft included kayaks, Canadian canoes, a Drascombe Lugger daysailer, a Wayfarer sailing dinghy and special yachts designed for solo use by disabled individuals.

On returning home, a compulsion to make further enquiries eventually led me to becoming a resident voluntary instructor during the summer months for the next several years. I had been motivated by a naïve sense of sharing my skills and experiences in an altruistic way, only to find that the extraordinary people who stayed at the Centre enriched me far more in return.

The Centre stands alone in an elevated position, with a westward prospect across the lake. On my initial arrival in my vintage yellow VW Polo, complete with touring bicycle on the back, I was cordially greeted by the Warden, Peter Lingard. Before long, I was seated in the driving seat next to him and the senior instructor in one of the mushroom-coloured 'ambulances' used for transporting guests on the various adventures throughout the district. I was to be given a proving driving test and soon found myself heading back towards Keswick and the convolutions of its inner roadways. I passed muster and, thanks to the practised and welcoming ethos of the Centre, was soon made to feel at home.

I was to discover the calibre of the youthful-looking instructors, who were not only highly skilled in their outdoor pursuits but rose to the additional challenges of enabling the best experiences for the visitors, who had to grapple with serious physical or mental complications. The instructors fell-ran to Skiddaw summit and back before breakfast, tested themselves with triathlon contests, were active members of the local Mountain Rescue Team, then switched adeptly to roping clients in wheelchairs to abseil down the graded rock slope descents at nearby St. John's in the Vale or, occasionally, off the dizzying heights of the mighty 'coathanger' bridge across the Tyne, at Newcastle.

I was engaged principally to assist with the water activities but, in successive years, was entrusted with my own 'ambulance' and groups, for a wider range of activities. My initiation was mentored by Nick Ball, whose humour and canniness was inspirational.

As the various teams assembled on the forecourt in the morning sunshine, behind the row

A day of zephyrs on Bassenthwaite Lake in the Lake District, at the Calvert Trust Adventure Centre for Disabled People.

of waiting vehicles with their boarding ramps ready to accept those in wheelchairs, the colourful bustle of the day began. A mischievous group of Down's Syndrome folk made a merry party for heading to the lake. A mile's drive along the road that skirts the eastern shore of the lake found us turning sharply onto a track across pastureland and through woodland to a substantial wooden boathouse reminiscent, for the romantically inclined, of a trapper's lonely cabin in the Canadian outback. Inside, indeed, were a goodly number of well-used open Canadian canoes, sharing the space with kayaks and all their paraphernalia. At moorings beyond, a safety boat dory and the daysailer took on an air of expectation, as the group enthusiastically disembarked onto the pebbly lake shore. For them, this week would mark an anticipated highlight of their year.

Soon a miscellany of craft lay at the waters' edge, their bows being lapped gently by the run of wavelets from the wind that scuffed the broad expanse of lake beyond the shelter of the shore. Like any other mountain-girt expanse of water or sea loch, the winds can be fickle, contrary and mischievous: an interesting playground for those afloat.

Pairs of Canadian canoes were cross-braced with lashed pine logs, to create stable platforms for the more uninitiated; single kayaks were filled by young folk who quitted their wheelchairs and, with compensatory upper body strength, became veritable ducks on the water.

The Drascombe Lugger was brought from its mooring to the jetty for embarkation of a small group of 'crew'. The boat was not dissimilar to my Cornish Coble, but carried an additional mizzen sail. The rig proved beneficial both for the varied conditions and the range of capabilities of the 'crew'. Sudden changes in wind strength could be reacted to rapidly, by dropping the mainsail, relying on jib and mizzen to remove the unease that can arise. Enjoyment was the watchword, although there was no shortage of the adventurous spirit either.

Just as the young Wordsworth observed disconcertedly in his poem *The Stolen Boat*, the sudden revelation of up-rearing silhouetted mountains as the rowing boat he guiltily procured cleared the wooded shores of another notable Lakeland water, so, too, the local peaks that flanked Bassenthwaite began to reveal themselves: mighty Skiddaw and Ullock Pike and the nearer peak of Dodd with its raiment of dark plantation woods. The shoreline and hinterland also drew the eye to historic manmade features. In its own mixed woodland, the estate of Mirehouse has formal associations with the Calvert Trust, providing an assault course and access to its gardens. In 1835 Alfred Lord Tennyson stayed here whilst he was writing *Morte D'Arthur*. Its opening lines were inspired by the little lakeside church of St. Bega's, in the grounds of the house: *… to a chapel nigh the field/A broken chancel with a broken cross,/That stood on a dark strait of barren land, …*

Devotees of the TV series *The Casebook of Sherlock Holmes,* starring Jeremy Brett, will recall the episode 'The Disappearance of Lady F Carfax.' It was to St. Bega's that she sailed herself across the lake to attend Sunday service, and nearly came to grief on her return journey. A happier and more recent occasion at the church was the marriage of two Calvert Trust instructors.

A favoured picnic spot for the groups near to the boathouse was at a simple open-air theatre created by the Tennyson Society, to mark the place where the poet is thought to have penned much of his celebrated poem. Here, recovered multiple-transplant patients laughingly compared scars, and spinal injury cases – both paraplegic and quadriplegic – often had the group in stitches of mirth.

Other locations were to be used on the grassy swards across the lake, beneath the watchful

Lunch break on the western shores of Bassenthwaite.

bulk of Barf, another peak with associations with the Trust. I was to find myself seconded as an observer during one of the Trust's in-house triathlons; a modified event, which was a great test of stamina and endurance. Participants ran from the Centre to the lake, across which they swam; then to fell-run the steep defiles to the summit of Barf, where I duly observed their progress and issued water. After the descent, there was a cycle of several miles back to the start. The winner completed the circuit in less than an hour.

Towards the northern end of Bassenthwaite a long-established private sailing club, which proudly shares its name with that of the lake, provides its members with the privilege of using the lake waters for sport. No motorized craft are permitted on the waters of this glorious setting, except for rescue purposes. A forthcoming major race meeting provided me with the opportunity to deliver the Trust's own 'safety' dory, to augment the club's own craft. On a still, warm and sunny late afternoon, it was a treat to combine legitimate work with the delicious pleasure of a private and sometimes sedate passage out of the mountainous surroundings into the more gentle landscapes at the far end of the lake, before berthing at the jetty and returning by road.

Drawn up in the dinghy park was a range of sailing craft, including Flying Fifteens and Wayfarers. The latter were known to me largely through the adventure writings of Frank and Margaret Dye, who famously took their Wayfarer, *Wanderer,* cruising across open seas from Scotland to Iceland, and to Norway, in the 1960s. At the time of reading, the idea seemed both exhilarating and rash, but success in both ventures proved the resilience of crew and boat alike. It was therefore with keen anticipation that I was soon to take charge of the Trust's Wayfarer with an appropriate group with adventurous spirit: courageous and humbling individuals who suffered from cystic fibrosis and who were determined to make the most of their young lives.

Thankfully, sailing conditions were kind: a moderate breeze from a direction which gave a good fetch of clear wind. As a large centreboard dinghy, with the potential for capsize, to a first-time user with crew who were implicitly placing their pleasure and safety in my hands, my looks hopefully disguised my concerns as we cast off from our own jetty. The boat, and her enthusiastic crew, provided a fresh and increasingly pleasurable sail. The hard boom of the mainsail was a new challenge for them, as opposed to the forgiving soft foot of its counterpart in the lugger: likewise the tucking of toes under the foot-straps and leaning outwards from the gunwales with nothing but fizzing water beneath the nether regions as the taut mass of white sail heeled the boat, brought exclamations of delight.

Thus initiated to the ways of a Wayfarer, it was with more confidence that I warmed to the suggestion by a good friend from infant school days onwards, to hire a Wayfarer for a sail on

Windermere. We had sailed together in the Mirror dinghy at Tynemouth and in the intervening years Paul and his wife Sue had gone on to take RYA dinghy sailing courses. Our afternoon sail on Windermere was a more advanced session, made the more satisfying with a 'competent crew'. The lake was busy with much traffic and the wind had all three of us at full stretch whilst beating to windward. I discovered the effects of 'excessive weather helm' – the tendency of the sails to pull the boat into the wind, especially when they are close hauled. A desirable trait in small measure and preferable to 'lee helm' which has the opposite effect, in excess it makes steering a challenge. Caused by the mast being raked too far aft by the supporting side shrouds, I found myself gritting my teeth to keep the rudder, with its lengthy tiller-extension, angled against the pull of the sails. Making any alteration of course downwind was almost impossible without easing the mainsail first. It may have been a deliberate action by the hirer, in case the occupants found themselves displaced from the moving boat. The Wayfarer would then have promptly stopped, head-to-wind, as opposed to careering off out of control downwind, if the sailing rig was set with lee-helm. In any event, it was a fine demonstration of the effect and need for 'tuning' even a simple sailing rig.

The author samples his brother's sailboard.

An even more basic rig is that of the single-sail Topper dinghy. I had acquired one second-hand, tempted by its ease of carriage on a car roof rack and for satisfying single-handed sailing. Early on, my brother, who had become a keen sailboarder, swapped craft at a large manmade lake at Killingworth on Tyneside, to try them out. Afterwards, I elected to continue with boats, as opposed to boards.

I took the Topper to the Calvert Trust for extra-curriculum use and was able to lend it to James Spedding, son of the Mirehouse estate, who often helped out with the activities of the Trust.

BOATS YET SAILING

The author's Topper is taken for a spin by James Spedding, of the Mirehouse estate, on the shores of Lake Bassenthwaite.

At the end of my final year's association as a resident voluntary instructor, James and I obtained permission to take the Drascombe Lugger out solo on the lake. Unshackled by the constraints of customer comfort, and in gusty, rain-squall conditions we put the boat – and ourselves – through our paces. Exchanging places at the helm, it was indeed a memorable 'thrash' and a fitting way to take my leave of such a fine organization. Having earlier sold my Topper in the Lake District, my roof rack was fortuitously vacant to receive the generous gift of one of the Trust's fibreglass Canadian canoes, which were being replaced by new stock. That boat remains with me to this day. Having seen much use on varied waters, it introduced a new generation of family to the pleasures and subtle techniques of properly wielding a Grey Owl paddle. It remains ready to embark the newest generation: young grandson Jack.

The gift of a former Calvert Trust canoe was put to later good use by the family; here on Ullswater: daughter Katy and my wife, Karen.

BOATS YET SAILING

KETCHES OF CHARACTER: THE OCEAN YOUTH CLUB

The Ocean Youth Club – OYC – came into being in 1960, with the founding principle of providing adventure at sea for young people from all parts of the United Kingdom. Its stated aims included: giving young people between the ages of 15 and 21 the opportunity to go to sea offshore, under sail; to foster the spirit of adventure latent in young people; inculcate a sense of responsibility among young people both for themselves and for others; to encourage a wider outlook and greater understanding of other people; to use a sailing ship as a classroom and the sea as a teacher …

Throughout the first decade, by necessity a number of 'old gaffer' sailing vessels were used, but by 1970 it was realized that a modern fleet of craft was needed. 'Freeman's Wharf', near Penryn in Cornwall was acquired by the OYC for construction of the fibreglass hulled yachts, the first of which became the longest production fibreglass sailing vessel in the world. Later, in 1973, *Samuel Whitbread* was launched.

*

More than a decade had passed since I sailed as a trainee on the Sail Training Schooner *Sir Winston Churchill*. In the intervening period I had been a full time navigating officer in the Merchant Navy before, in 1985, taking what turned out to be a break of four years. In a position to offer my services as a volunteer in a range of 'outdoor pursuits', I took advantage of a formal arrangement of the OYC to recruit potential watch leaders on their sail training yachts. As I was based in the northeast of England on Tyneside, I was aware that the organization was upgrading its fleet with new designs, to succeed earlier craft. The new local yacht – to be called *James Cook* – was under construction on Tyneside, at a yard which encouraged trainees and apprentices in the industry.

A suitable individual was permitted two 'training voyages' as a participating supernumerary on scheduled cruises. Anticipating the commissioning of *James Cook,* I secured a position on a forthcoming voyage, with a view to a follow-up on the same boat, in order to become thoroughly familiar with its operation. However, because of initial and then on-going issues with *James Cook*, requiring its periodic removal from service, I carried out the two training voyages on different classic yachts: both of great character and reputation. The first was *Samuel Whitbread*.

*

The Port of Blyth had been the erstwhile storage place for my Cornish Coble and before that an often visited location to observe the maritime scene. In the 1960s Blyth was the biggest coal-exporting town in Europe. Much of its success was owed to the huge wooden coal staithes which enabled coal from the nearby pits to be transported and loaded onto awaiting colliers direct from railway wagons. These staithes were featured in the 1971 film *Get Carter*, starring Michael Caine. To teenage eyes, the clattering black-dusty spectacle of steam-hauled coal wagons discharging into colliers and flatirons, which frequently sailed for destinations in London and beyond, was thrilling. Likewise, a visit to South Harbour, which bustled with fishing craft and pleasure yachts. Base for the Royal Northumberland Yacht Club, its floating clubhouse is a rare wooden Trinity House lightvessel, still functioning today.

Many years into the future, it was here that *Samuel Whitbread* was berthed, ready to embark not only young trainees, but myself as an older Jolly Jack: as a trainee watch leader, mentor and motivator for those same expectant individuals.

An added bonus was voyaging in home waters, seeing stretches of coast familiar from the shore, and from the low and quiet vantage of a fine sailing vessel, sharing the experiences through the fresh eyes of our companion crew, who embraced their roles with enthusiasm and increasing confidence, under the guidance of the skipper Ron Lovelady and his competent watchkeepers. I, too, was attentive to my own role, equally absorbed in learning the ropes and later in the trip, to assume watches under supervision.

The departure from Blyth had a palpable feel of following in the footsteps of the countless

On the Ocean Youth Club ketch *Samuel Whitbread*, the young trainees receive initial familiarization.

BOATS YET SAILING

colliers of yesteryear, but heading northwards instead. We were to be blest with moderate prevailing westerly winds offshore, perfect for speedy and comfortable sailing, and with settled nights. On Scotland's East Lothian coast, the town of Dunbar with its substantial historic harbour was the initial destination. Anchoring off its narrow entrance channel for the night, a run ashore by boat gradually revealed a dramatic approach, beneath the towering castle ruins and red sandstone cliffs, bedecked with the circling activity and raucous calling of many nesting kittiwakes. Departure next morning was by dint of many hands, as anchor was weighed as a manual team effort.

The outer reaches of the Firth of Tay, in the vicinity of Tayport on the southern shore, was our next destination, crossing the wide sleeve of the Firth of Forth.

Above: All hands to weighing anchor, off Dunbar.
Below: A different perspective of *Samuel Whitbread*.

Two lighthouse structures upstream of Tayport provided useful marks by which to moor and monitor our anchorage position; a visit to the lofty head of the mainmast offering a different perspective, before beginning to retrace our steps southwards next day, under full sail.

I was excited at the prospect for the day, terminating at Tweedmouth, the environs of my own first dwelling. Having previously witnessed from the long entrance pier the comings and goings of commercial coasters negotiating the sinuous narrow channel into the River Tweed, the experience was completed by transiting it aboard *Samuel Whitbread,* and berthing in the compact commercial dock itself. Departing from here the next morning was a masterful demonstration by the skipper of having an intimate understanding of the yacht's manoeuvring capabilities under power. A stiff wind pinned the boat alongside, requiring maximum use of the technique known as springing off: retaining one mooring rope leading aft from forward, and using the full ahead thrust of the engine to 'lift' the stern away from the quay, before backing into the centre of the otherwise unoccupied dock. All the while the wind was having its effect, and a bold decision of full ahead and hard to port took the yacht in a tight but sliding arc, her rapidly swinging stern clearing the unforgiving dock sides by a close margin. Our exit into the Tweed was spectacular!

An invigorating breeze off the Northumberland coast.

Leaving behind the stocky white and red pier-end lighthouse, course was set towards the holy island of Lindisfarne, low on the horizon. It was to be a passage of much navigational interest, rounding the sand duned northeastern extremity of Emmanuel Head, for a southerly leg close to a rocky shore so as to pass 'inside' the hazard of Plough Rock: all the while the distinctive bulk of Lindisfarne Castle changed its uprearing aspect. Our anchorage was to be in the sheltered roads known simply as The Harbour. Getting there safely through outlying shoals required the careful use of two sets of leading marks. The first are two imposing chimney-like stone towers, looking black against the low skyline. These provide a safe westward

BOATS YET SAILING

The powerful sail training ketch *Halcyon*, of Warsash College, was seconded to the Ocean Youth Club.

THE COLLEGE OF NAUTICAL STUDIES

Warsash, Southampton

Sail Training Vessel

"HALCYON"

Left: All trainees took 'tricks' at the wheel.

Below: In Dundee, the backdrop of RRS *Discovery* was an inspiration, as the trainees bent on *Halcyon*'s mainsail.

KETCHES OF CHARACTER: THE OCEAN YOUTH CLUB

…going well.

Close-hauled on port tack, *Halcyon* thunders southwards off the Lothian shore.

105

A senior lecturer at Warsash Marine College, *Halcyon*'s redoubtable skipper was a firm but fair taskmaster.

passage until a different set of marks towards the Benedictine priory led us through Burrows Hole, which is bounded by submerged shingle banks. There was a sense of achievement, once more – and another notable and historic location to spend the final night before our return and disbanding at Blyth. Everybody aboard had acquitted themselves well: the trainees would have learned much more than the art of sailing: that was also the case for me. It was to be another year before I took up my next voyage with the OYC. *James Cook* eluded me for a second time: *Halcyon* proved to be a memorable substitute.

*

The itinerary and stamping ground for the voyage was necessarily similar to that of *Samuel Whitbread*, heading northwards again. The east coast is relatively devoid of islands as compared to the West Coast of Scotland, but notable individual examples nevertheless provided interest in their passing: Coquet Island; the Farne Islands of Grace Darling fame; Holy Island; in the Firth of Forth excursions were made in the vicinity of Bass Rock and The Isle of May.

Our furthest north was to the port of Dundee, with an overnight berth adjacent to a treasured and potent monument not only of a great sailing tradition, but of British polar exploration and discovery. Once more at the city where she was built, the Royal Research Ship *Discovery*, best known for taking Captain Scott and Ernest Shackleton on their highly successful expedition to the Antarctic at the beginning of the 20th century, could not but be an inspiration. Quietly for me, as I had already served as an officer on both the latest Royal Research Ships – *Discovery*, and *Shackleton*. They kept up the tradition of the original, as the first ever to be designated as an 'RRS' – Royal Research Ship.

A highlight of the voyage was an overnight passage southwards from the Firth of Forth, again with a helpful and exhilarating offshore breeze. Assigned a watch of my own, the usual thrill was tempered by slight anxiety: under full sail, a starry night and the slight red and green loom of the side lights, there was still the feeling of how easily order could become chaos. I was, after all, not yet an expert! Character building is as much taking on a challenge, as it is for the instructor to place his trust whilst occupying a discreet berth below.

Already nearly sixty years old, *Halcyon* was a venerable, powerful and capable vessel and revelled in being driven to her capabilities by her skipper, a senior lecturer at Warsash College of Nautical Studies. He was the embodiment of a master mariner, exhibiting a firm kindness and example to all his charges, providing both enduring and inspirational memories to draw on in later life. *Halcyon* very soon afterwards completed her final voyage as a training vessel, reverting thereafter to private ownership.

*

Prior to the millennium, my teenage daughter Katy did catch up with *James Cook*, sailing as a trainee, creating a modern family tradition. Recently, her own young son, Jack, has already looked admiringly on *James Cook* at her home berth in North Shields, and likewise at his mother who, as is the way of such things, may have induced a latent sense of his own adventure to come.

Grandson Jack is shown *James Cook* by his grandmother. His mother had been a trainee on this OYC yacht as a teenager.

BOATS YET SAILING

WHITE MOTH – SKIPPERED WHERRY YACHT

SLEEPS UP TO 10

At the turn of the century, Wherry yachts were the ultimate in luxury to Edwardians seeking an adventure holiday on the Broads

Commissioned in 1915 and entirely re-fitted by local craftsmen, she is one of the last examples of her kind, providing an idyllic means of experiencing the beautiful Norfolk Broads. Sailing this elegant craft is a unique way of enjoying the variety of wildlife and scenery, as well as providing an insight into how the Edwardians spent their time on the Broads. A skipper and local guide is in charge of the day-to-day running of the craft (self-contained crew quarters are situated in the forepeak) and you may sail the boat just as much or as little as you wish. The Wherry sleeps up to ten guests in three double cabins and two double settee berths. Our Wherry is ideal for re-living an Edwardian holiday

- Each cabin has a wash basin with hot and cold water
- Two separate toilet/shower compartments
- Central heating
- Opulently furnished saloon with full-size dining table
- Galley with four burner hob, grill, oven and large fridge

Regret no all male/all female groups unless with prior permission

Will not pass under Potter Heigham bridge

Rig Gaff with single loose-footed mainsail of over 1000 square feet

Engine Inboard diesel for full motor cruising capability

5 doubles with 2 toilets & 2 showers
Length: 59ft (17.98m) Beam: 13ft 6in (4.11m)
Headroom 6ft (1.83m) decreasing aft

EXAMPLE COSTS

FRIDAY 5PM - SUNDAY 5PM	£814
FOR 2 DAYS: WEEKDAY 5PM - WEEKDAY 5PM	£689
7 NIGHTS 5PM - 9AM	£1656
MON/THURS DAY CRUISE	£363

up to 10% less from October to March (inclusive) other variations on request. Prices inclusive of cancellation protection. Fuel, Gas and bedding are all included.

AVAILABLE FOR ANY START DAY
FOR CRUISES OF ANY DURATION
REF BBC50

The entry for the skippered wherry yacht *White Moth*, in a 2004 Yachting Holidays brochure.

WHITE MOTH A-BROAD

The prospect was irresistible: the opportunity not only to explore the incomparable inland waters of the Norfolk Broads, but to do so by helping to 'work' a rare vintage Wherry yacht and to study the water- and landscapes on a formal watercolour painting holiday: reliving pastimes of the Edwardian era.

White Moth is a Wherry yacht listed in the National Historic Ships Register. Built in 1915 in the Norfolk Broads at Wroxham for a private owner, she has had a chequered history. In the mid-1980s she was saved from destruction and after four years of restoration, aimed at the hire market, she has operated as a charter vessel.

*

Making the long but familiar drive south towards East Anglia, the car boot was packed with additional items, as per the instructions from our art tutor. As an established amateur dabbler, I was already equipped with most of the requirements and I looked forward to the impetus that a shared course can induce. Many musings behind the wheel helped with the journey: who would be my fellow students – and what are their stories and how would we integrate in a confined space? Likewise, that of our tutor? What will the subject matter consist? Our skipper? Accommodation and meals? The realities of sailing *White Moth*? The weather and its consequences?

The Wherry's home base was at Horning, an ancient village close to where I had previously worked at the boatyard of Jack Chippendale, in Wroxham. Horning is a quintessential Broadlands settlement, lining one side of the River Bure which arced in a dramatic hair-pin bend. *White Moth* was nestled in a covered berth, and became the focus for sundry arrivals, all bearing the tell-tale accoutrements of artistic endeavour and cruising.

The 'crew' appeared to be mostly 'of an age' and seemed intent on having a pleasant time. We were all impressed by the quiet grace of the boat, her rich wooden

BOATS YET SAILING

WHITE MOTH A-BROAD

interior exuding character and quality. Our skipper, too, was jovial and his broad stature and ruddy complexion beneath a white bush hat suggested he carried his command in a capable and easy-going manner.

Edging out of the dock into the river, in light airs the mighty sail was raised and we felt the first silent stirrings and pull of the boat. The coming days were to pass in an unhurried, magical way; seemingly stepping out of the present for a glimpse back to the time of the Edwardians who took to the same waters to indulge in similar pursuits.

Our tutor, knowledgeable in the subject matter, which would make good watercolour subjects, took us to a variety of locations. Getting to each of them was of course a large ingredient, in which the helm and mainsheet of the sail was given over to anyone who wished to steer this wonderful yacht, under the watchful eye and guidance of the skipper. At other times, in light airs or when a low bridge had to be negotiated, requiring the lowering of the massive mast, the inboard engine purred softly. Occasionally, another traditional method of manoeuvring was practised – that of the quant.

Popularized in the saying 'I wouldn't touch it with a barge pole', the quant is indeed a lengthy wooden pole which is used to propel such a boat, or manoeuvre in tight spaces. *White Moth's* quant was substantial, with a button at one end to prevent it from sinking into the soft bed of river or broad. Curiosity and a sense of fun found several crew exploring the technique and pleased at being able to so move such a substantial craft.

After dinner and tidying up, evenings were spent sketching or working on paintings, our tutor treating us to excellent demonstrations in the stillness of the saloon below deck, or on location. A highlight was a sail to study the singular ruins of St. Benet's Abbey, at Hulme. Tying up on the opposite bank of the river, we beheld the venerable structure in its solitary setting. Rearing up from inside the ruins was the conical remains of a windmill, added at a later date. The Bishop of Norwich continues to be Abbot of this Abbey.

Our river berth also coincided with the junction of a substantial cut, Fleet Dyke, leading to South Walsham Broad. The yacht's boat could be rigged with a single blue sail and was deployed for the amusement of skipper and guests, sailing single handed. In the light airs, the set of the sail did not allow for the certainty of tacking: the boat generally ending up 'in irons' – not able to pass through the eye of the wind before coming to a halt – requiring the use of a paddle to complete the manoeuvre: a not uncommon drawback of such a single sail.

All of a sudden it was the final night, and a finale: a meal ashore at a restaurant. Repairing to *White Moth* in the twilight, also at the request of our tutor to bring along some form of party piece, I recited what I felt would be both an homage to the wonderful week, but also a plea for the preservation of all wild and wet places, the poem *Inversnaid*, by Gerard Manly Hopkins, the final stanza of which reads:

What would the world be, once bereft
Of wet and of wildness? Let them be left,
O let them be left, wildness and wet;
Long live the weeds and the wilderness yet.

BOATS YET SAILING

A FLEET WORTH HUNTING

The enduring and inspirational 'Swallows & Amazons' writings of Arthur Ransome, which enhanced the family visits across the high Pennines from Tyneside to the magical realm of the Lake District, echoed down the years to that other entrancing water-world of the Norfolk Broads, the location for his tales of adventure, *Coot Club,* and *The Big Six.*

The BBC Television adaptations of these books used local boats in starring roles. They were sourced from the then Norfolk County Sailing Base at Ludham. The yacht which featured as *Teasel* was actually one of the Sailing Base's craft – *Lullaby*. She was fitted for her new role with a false transom, bearing the new name and registry of Ludham.

On the outskirts of Ludham village, down a meandering tree-lined lane, which supports protected banks of blooming wild flowers, the two traditional boat sheds of Hunter's Yard nestle comfortably into the gentle landscape at the head of an exclusive dyke of water. This is home to the same unique fleet of pure sailing craft. Most of the bright varnished mahogany gaff sloops were built in the 1930s. They are in pristine condition; testimony to the craftsmanship and ongoing care of professional boatbuilders and sailing enthusiasts alike. They provide a truly timeless experience. One of the boats is *Lullaby.*

In 1996, the Norfolk Heritage Fleet Trust was set up to ensure a thriving future for the pre-existing fleet, to uphold the boatbuilding skills and traditions of the original and reinstated Hunter's Yard and to encourage youth sailing. In the spring of 2001 the first new cabin yacht to be built at the yard since 1949 was commenced. Visitors to the yard continue to be openly welcomed into the hallowed and dimly-lit sheds. The scents of wood shavings and varnish would have excited the imagination, adding to the visual spectacle of the new boat's hull slowly evolving about its uncanny skeletal symmetry.

As Easter marks the start of the hire season, the boats were slipped once more into their element. Joined by a few rare examples of traditional wooden half-deckers that serve equally well as day boats or camping boats for the more adventurous, the small dedicated team take immense satisfaction from their labours of winter. The brochure for 2002 quietly and accurately reflected the yard's qualities: it was the only Broads hire fleet that still had no engines and no electricity – environmentally friendly hire yachts that people come back to time and again;

beautiful boats which sail superbly well. As a supporting Friend of the fleet, I was about to discover that for myself.

*

'Hello! – my name is Ian; I'm going with you … Yes, it is my day off, but I fancy a good sail …!' This was a good omen and typical of the old-fashioned and friendly courtesy freely given.

Moored alongside was *Hustler V*, one of the boats capable of sleeping three people. In the sheltered dyke only zephyrs rippled the surface. The rasping of tree tops hinted at a more substantial and steady breeze out on nearby Womack Water. With a knowing glance at the near-cloudless sky, Ian indicated that he had already put a single reef in the mainsail.

Casting off, with sails yet unhoisted, we drifted slowly with the wind's unseen hand, aided by tiller and the long quanting pole. Sinking softly into the ooze it was our main manoeuvring propulsion. At the entrance to the dyke, we 'weather-vaned' onto the upwind knuckle, lying head-to-wind and secured at the bow. 'We hoist the jib first. It pulls the mast forward and gives an extra six inches headroom in the cockpit … If you hoist the throat of the mainsail, I'll do the peak.'

Without fuss the four-sided sail was raised and set. I've known sailing dinghies far more complicated and, as it was to turn out, far less responsive. – just one of the qualifying joys of not having the dead weight ballast of an inboard engine and fuel tanks.

An historic sailing base on the Norfolk Broads: Hunter's Yard, Ludham.

Running before the chill north-westerly breeze *Hustler* good-naturedly carried us to the junction with the Thurne and the mile-long graceful curve of that river which allowed our craft to impress with her romping abilities in a beam wind.

'Because of the sail shape she carries a deal of weather helm when close hauled'. Zipping up his fleece, Ian conveyed this timely advice

Friends of The Hunter Fleet
Norfolk Heritage Fleet Trust
Registered Charity No. 1052303

Hunter's Yard, Horsefen Road, Ludham, NR29 5QG
Tel: 01692 678263 - 01455 203167
www.huntersyard.co.uk

BOATS YET SAILING

The author enjoyed a two-hour skippered sail, whilst on a course at Lowestoft Marine College.

before we exited Thurne Mouth onto the substantial waterway that is the River Dune. The next two glorious miles of sinewy all-but-deserted reaches offered a grand testing ground to get that all-important 'feel' beneath the feet. The short tiller was not skitty and paranoid like that of some dinghies, but firm, positive and forgiving. Ian was right in his warning: the gusts hauled the bow automatically closer into the wind with a living surge of power from above. At the masthead, the tricolour burgee was our trusty and low-tech wind sensor, adding to the feel on the cheek and to confirm the tell-tale back-billowing of a sail that needed adjustment.

The boisterous breeze crossed the low tracts of fenland unhindered. Above the banks of golden reeds the extraordinary isolated ruins of St. Benet's Abbey compelled the eyes to gaze. No sooner passed than a direct run southwards again along the narrowing Fleet Dyke bore us towards flanking woodland and a delightful constriction into the shimmering and sheltered waters of South Walsham Broad. Apparently denied at any time to motorized craft, this jewel has rightly been described as pure Swallows and Amazons. On this day it embodied and evoked those youthful adventures of Arthur Ransome's enduring characters.

'I've never come as far as this on a test sail,' Ian gleefully remarked. 'It's a personal record!' Not being one for wittingly setting records, but it had been a superb 'thrash'; and there was still the return journey … Fleet Dyke now presented a graded challenge. The funnelling wind ran directly down its length, necessitating ten-second zigzags and tacks at either bank. *Hustler* handled like a dream. She excelled in her natural homeland, carrying way into and through the wind's eye with never a hint of stalling. As the stern whispered past the reeds, nesting coot merely tilted their heads in mute response; grebes did not pause in their waterborne courtships and swans anticipated our moves with faultless grace. With no option of a motor, senses quickly sharpened to anticipate and adequately provide answers to those questions of what if?

Relieving at the tiller, Ian proved his consummate skills with an ease that brings ready admiration from any mariner. With trepidation he said he was going to night class to learn about crewing a yacht at sea. 'I've never been on the coast before.'

It was now my turn to reassure and salve his own ill-founded self-doubts: 'Catastrophic things occasionally do happen at sea, but – as with me here – its about making mistakes and learning from them'.

A DELAYED DATE WITH *CHRISTINA*

The author John Seymour is perhaps best remembered for his seminal publication *The Complete Book of Self Sufficiency,* in which he advocated a lifestyle lived as close to nature as possible. First published in 1976 it has been described as a vital resource for disillusioned city dwellers seeking a more wholesome existence in the countryside. In this he was an ecological pioneer. For a time, after WWII he worked on one of the last sailing barges on the east and south coasts.

In the early 1970s John Seymour had moved with his family to a farm near Newport, Pembrokeshire in West Wales. The farm became something of a mecca for devotees of his philosophy of simple living. At the time of the publication of his book about self-sufficiency I was twenty years old and an avid reader of its contents. I resolved to journey to Pembrokeshire and did indeed benefit from a stay at the farm.

Taking advantage of being in that part of the world for the first time, I explored the local coasts and made what was to be an extraordinary discovery: one which I would not fully appreciate for a further thirty years. Drawn up on a grassy backdrop to a sandy foreshore, a beautiful example of a sailing coble sat alone and comfortably on the short-cropped sward. The brightwork of her varnished exterior glistened in the sun and her sailing spars sat neatly across her thwarts. Seen from a distance, I excitedly wondered if this might be John Seymour's famous sailing coble *Willynilly*, in which he and a companion voyaged across the North Sea into foreign waters, and which stars in his book *Willynilly to the Baltic:* a memorable tale. When he saw a fleet of Yorkshire cobles running in from the sea he decided there and then – willynilly – to acquire one. Coincidentally, at about the same time I had made approaches to a famous coble builder at Amble in Northumberland, to explore the possibility of ordering a new mini sailing coble. I had been inspired by examples of sailing cobles, seen moored at Whitby. I was taken seriously and learned a great deal from the experience. Expense was the limiting factor which led me eventually to acquire a modern fibreglass equivalent – *Chilawee*.

The coble I saw turned out to have the unusual name *White Maa*. She became a subject for my camera and several pictures continue to occupy a familiar place in my personal albums of traditional boats of Britain. It was not until well after the millennium that I unknowingly met up again with *White Maa*. This time the boat was in my own home waters – actually berthed in the marina at Royal Quays, in North Shields. This is the former location of Tyne Commission Quay where the classic liners serving Norway used to berth: my first job afloat, as an occasional after-school baggage porter.

Latterly, as a member of the Coble & Keelboat Society, which, for over thirty years, has researched and preserved the history of the 'Coble Coast' – from Berwick-upon-Tweed to the Humber – I was invited to join Frank Taylor, the owner of a sailing coble, for a sail out onto the River Tyne. In the course of conversation at his home, I happened to recall my historic sighting of *White Maa*. A slow smile preceded the intelligence that his coble – *Christina* – used to be *White Maa* …!

On a family holiday, in Whitby harbour a beautiful sailing coble was an early inspiration to the author.

To the incredulous who consider such coincidences impossible, I can verify the seafaring veracity of the uncanny close-quarter convergence of individual ships in mid-ocean, following entirely different routes. I relished this particular version, and the prospect of a sail in this enigmatic coble was indeed a thrill.

The banks of the lower reaches of the River Tyne have been transformed from their many traditional roles in support of a bustling and major commercial port. Shipyard docks have been in-filled and their surrounding environments encrusted with desirable apartment blocks. The former Tyne Commission Quay with its direct boat-train links, which serviced the Norwegian ferries and its hinterland dock basin, are likewise a setting for a substantial marina of encompassing housing, the owners of which have the privilege of hearing the insistent discordant chiming of halyards against the hollow metal masts of an array of yachts. Sitting quietly at her pontoon berth amidst the anonymous fibreglass sailing craft and weekend rod-fishing boats, *Christina* was a jewel. The maroon paint defined her elegant form, the rich creamy interior was inviting and the rake of the wooden mast was a diagonal of latent intent and drama.

The only boat to use the lock out of the basin, as the water level dropped, Frank introduced me to the niceties of the rig and the exercise it took to deploy the bowsprit and raise the sails. There was quiet water on exiting the lock, as use was made of the handy little interior motor, but the run of the tide and the scuff of a good breeze blowing directly up river from the sharp bend upstream of North Shields Fish Quay, gave hint of an interesting prospect. The long wooden tiller could be raised and lowered with a touch of the hand. Standing was an unusual but appropriate stance, the main sheet as ever gripped by the forward hand. As the touch of wind tautened the close-hauled expanse of sails, it was time to get 'the feel' of this example of a sailing craft I had known and loved mainly from afar. She exceeded expectation!

The flood tide negated the current of the river and the free wind fetched steadily up the broad reach of water. In consequence, it turned out that little upwind headway could be made downstream, but the criss-cross tacks gave ample scope to experience and appreciate the handling qualities in what was a fine breeze. Gingerly at first, both luffing up in gusts and easing the sheets as the boat heeled, experiment kept the sheet close hauled, enabling the wonderful rounded tumblehome shape of the hull aft to compensate. Yet aware of my novice status and in the public arena of the river, as well as the privilege given me by Frank, prudence prevailed

Whilst attending a self-sufficiency course at John Seymour's establishment in Pembrokeshire, the chance discovery of the sailing coble *White Maa* translated many years into the future as *Christina*...

Photo: Adrian Don/ElectricPics Photography

over daring. Some ground was gained, allowing for both a satisfying reach and running before the wind; the last ringing warnings about this point of sailing being perhaps the weak spot in the hull's design, with little grip aft, save for the very deep rudder.

As we returned towards the lock I reflected how *Christina* must have looked from unseen eyes on the banks: the sole local representative of her type, displaying a romantic reminder of the past when the fleets sailed out from Cullercoats and other Fair Havens on the Coble Coast.

…which the author was invited to crew and sail on the River Tyne, by her then owner Frank Taylor. Here, the coble is seen taking part in the 2006 Harbour Day, at Cullercoats: the author had come 'full circle'!

MUSINGS AT THE MOORINGS

Two traditionally significant birthdays occur in the 60s: namely the 60th and the 65th, although these days the latter can no longer be officially linked with 'retirement age'. However, the concept of Retirement as life beyond the necessity of earning a living full time can mark an era of new opportunities, or in some ways to reinvigorate or adapt old interests.

My 60th birthday inspired my wife Karen to buy me a wooden automaton kit; selecting one which combined my former love of model-making with that of sailing and boat-building. Five years later, for my 65th, the completed model inspired her knack for cake decoration. Keeping the display intact allowed grandson Jack to choose a cake topping for his own 5th birthday; the same sailing boat, but with the addition of a certain small crew. The tradition may be set to continue …

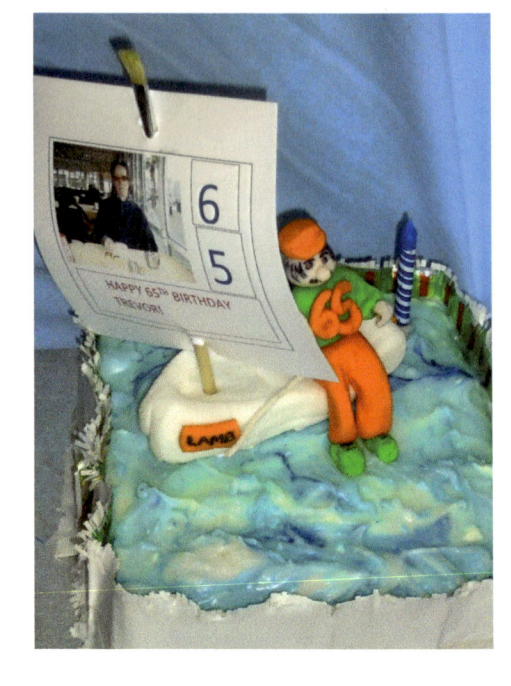

Right: A 60th birthday present of a timber kit automaton enabled the author to comfortably reconnect with his sailing and boatbuilding past…

Far right: …further celebrated – five years later – by a cake made by his wife, Karen.

BEYOND THE BOWSPRIT

Fairhaven Lake
The lake still provides a venue for dinghy sailing, with taster sessions and recognized courses being provided by a local sailing club.

Reflections of a Mirror
The Mirror has been described as the world's most popular double-handed sailing dinghy. The class continues to have a strong UK racing circuit as well as an international following. With 71,000 built, they are raced competitively worldwide and are a recommended UK Olympic pathway boat.

Tynemouth Sailing Club remains active and includes a fleet of single-handed racing dinghies as well as crewed boats. Ryton is no longer used as a venue for winter racing, due to changes in the fleet and local issues. Use is made of a nearby lake instead.

Corryvreckan Spins Yarns
Corryvreckan is considered the third largest tidal whirlpool in the world. Private and commercial boat trips to the Gulf of Corryvreckan are available.

A charter yacht called *Corryvreckan* continues the tradition of a predecessor, in offering cruising in the waters of Western Scotland.

A Sea-Worthy Association
The Sail Training Association became the Tall Ships Youth Trust in 2003 and is the oldest and largest sail training charity in the UK. In the millennium the schooner *Sir Winston Churchill*, together with her sister, completed their final voyages with the Association. They were replaced by two new-build brigs. The later acquisition of a large catamaran and a ketch augmented the Trust's ability to offer sailing experiences to younger age groups and to those with disabilities.

Chilawee & Chikanee

The boatbuilding firm of Cornish Crabbers is still based at Rock in Cornwall, producing high quality modern interpretations of classic sailing craft.

Remembering Bligh and Shackleton

Although modern ships' lifeboats are not designed primarily for making lengthy voyages, when sold out of original service they can be repurposed in many ways. Former lifeboats from the Western Isles passenger fleet of CalMac Ferries have been acquired as a houseboat, to further Africa's tourist industry, and as an expedition craft which, after lengthy conversion, was successfully used to explore the Norwegian coast and into the Arctic.

James Caird, the boat which made the incredible journey skippered by Ernest Shackleton is on display at the Laboratory at Dulwich College, London.

Boats Yet Sailing

Today, the training establishment at Oulton Broad continues as IBTC, but as a 'College' as opposed to a 'Centre'.

Richard Birmingham, former instructor at IBTC and whose book on boat building inspired the author to pursue the craft, is Professor of Small Craft Design at Newcastle University, and a former president of the Royal Institution of Naval Architects.

A Ranger and Shepherd go Forth

The Shetland-Fair Isle supply vessel *Good Shepherd IV* reached her 35th anniversary in May 2021.

A Priceless Chippendale in Wroxham

Wroxham Barns continues as a popular visitor attraction, hosting a range of working arts and crafts studios in which the public are invited to view the skills of local craftspeople: a lasting legacy of the centre's co-founders, one of which was Jack Chippendale.

Breezes on Bassenthwaite

In addition to the Calvert Trust in the Lake District, there are also centres at Kielder in Northumberland and Exmoor. The Lake District centre has further expanded in residential capacity and water activities.

Frank Dye's famous cruising Wayfarer, *Wanderer,* is exhibited at the National Maritime Museum, Falmouth.

Ketches of Character
The then skipper of *Samuel Whitbread*, Ron Lovelady, captained her in the last Tall Ships Race ever to sail from the Pool of London. (1989)

In the millennium, the Ocean Youth Club became the Ocean Youth Trust and operates in four independent regional areas of the UK. The OYT North training ketch is *James Cook*, based at North Shields.

Halcyon was built in 1929, acquired twenty eight years later by the Warsash School of Navigation in Southampton – a training establishment for the Merchant Navy. For thirty two years she proved highly successful as a training vessel for cadet officers before reverting to a private yacht. Given an impressive restoration and refit in 2004 *Halcyon* is now a luxury charter yacht.

White Moth A-Broad
In August 2020 the Bishop of Norwich, the Rt Revd Graham Usher, became the latest Patron of the charity Wherry Yacht Charter, which supports the preservation and use of the five Wherry yachts at the Norfolk Broads. The occasion was marked with his first trip aboard one of these craft for his journey to St. Benet's Abbey for the annual open-air service. The Bishop stated: '… *Jesus spoke from a boat to the listening crowds and taught about the water of life. I hope that I will be able to encourage and enable others to enjoy and experience the spiritual connection that can be found through exploring the waters and landscape of the Norfolk Broads on one of your five beautiful wherries.*'

A Fleet Worth Hunting
Hunter's Yard at Ludham is in the care of the Norfolk Heritage Fleet Trust. In 2020 it was decided to begin fitting engines to the majority of its historic wooden gaff sloops. As a charity, the trust enables many young people and adults to experience sailing for the first time, and offers a range of Keelboat Courses.

A Delayed Date with Christina
The Coble & Keelboat Society (CKS) has researched and preserved the history of the Coble Coast – from the River Tweed to the Humber. Amongst others, its members are fishermen,

authors, poets, artists, model makers and maritime historians. They have a wide interest in the maritime heritage of the North East and Yorkshire coasts. Individual members own sailing- and motor-cobles and other traditional local working craft.

In recent years, on the East Yorkshire coast, the Bridlington Sailing Coble Preservation Society (BSCPS) has staged an annual sailing coble festival. A two-day event, it draws increasing numbers of boats and admiring spectators. At sea, the boats create a dramatic visual spectacle whilst sailing in the bay. Nowhere else in Britain can a larger concentration of such historic sailing cobles been seen together. This has included *Christina*.

*

Selected inspirational books

Willynilly to the Baltic . . . . by John Seymour
Sailing Alone Around the World . . . . by Joshua Slocum
Innocent Aboard . . . . by Chay Blyth
Riddle of the Sands . . . . by Erskine Childers
The Falcon on the Baltic . . . . by E.F. Knight
Ocean Crossing Wayfarer . . . . by Frank & Margaret Dye
Country Living by Sea & Estuary . . . . by Suzanne Beedell
The Dinghy Cruising Companion . . . . by Roger Barnes
Boat Building Techniques Illustrated . . . . by [Prof] Richard Birmingham
A Boatbuilder's Story . . . . by Percy Mitchell
Schooner Master . . . . by Peter Carnahan
Clyde Cruising Club Sailing Directions: West Coast of Scotland

BIOGRAPHICAL NOTE

Sophie Neville learnt to sail dinghies at Newport Bay in Pembrokeshire, later making her own sail for a Thames skiff so she could take it down the lake where she grew up in Gloucestershire. Playing 'Titty' in the original film of *Swallows and Amazons* involved quite a bit of rowing which she kept up, first as a member of the Collingwood Ladies Four at Durham University and later on as the crew of *The Drapers' Shallop*, a ceremonial barge often spotted on the Thames and River Lea, the Dart or Poole Harbour. Her dedication to fixed thwart rowing enabled Sophie to take part in a Jubilee Pageant for the Queen at Henley, transport a copy of the Magna Carta to Windsor, and man an oar of the royal barge *Gloriana* in the Boat race flotilla at Putney in a year when Cambridge won. Belonging to the rowing club, *City Barge*, she has taken part in the *Voga Longa* in Venice, stood to row a sandalo down the Amstel to Amsterdam and navigate a shallop down a tributary of the Loire in Brittany, leading a procession of two hundred and forty traditional boats into Nantes for the *Rendez-vous de l'Erdre*.

Sophie grew up with boats in the garden. Her father, Martin Neville, owned eight at one time, including two coracles and a vintage launch called *Ottor*. While setting up a team that developed the fibreglass hull, he raced on the Solent, volunteered on a tall ship, and crossed the Atlantic on the maiden return voyage of the QE2, taking his daughter around the liner when it reached Southampton. While living in the City of London, he built a boat at Tower Hamlets, needing to remove a workshop window to lower it outside and onto a trailer. He took Sophie away from her wedding in a punt, while she sat with her new husband, holding an umbrella while a rainbow appeared over the water.

One of Sophie's favourite vessels is a two-man canvas canoe but she nearly drowned after getting stuck in a kayak and prefers an open dugout or fibreglass equivalent. These have taken her on adventures in Papua New Guinea, across Lake Malawi and through the Okavango Delta in Botswana. In 1978, Sophie helped her father to restore a 1901 steamboat called *Daffodil* which they kept near Oxford, at Port Meadow on the Thames. They would steam down to Henley each year for the royal regatta, or upstream towards Letchlade. In 1991, they took a Humber Yawl to take part in a Steam Boat Association rally on Windermere to pay homage to launches used in *Swallows and Amazons*, kept by George Pattinson at the Steam Boat Museum. Thirty years later, Sophie returned to Windermere Jetty with *Swallow's* pennant and other props from the film, to appear on BBC *Antiques Roadshow,* when the art expert Rupert Maas was able to sail *Swallow*.

While serving as President of The Arthur Ransome Society, Sophie has given a number of Q&A sessions at cinemas, giving families the chance to admire or sail the little clinker-built dinghy used as *Swallow*, which she helped SailRansome to purchase when the boat came up for auction in 2010. She has written numerous articles about her life afloat, spoken at literary festivals, on BBC Radio and nearly capsized on ITV News. It is with The Arthur Ransome Society that she has been able to sail an historic wherry on the Norfolk Broads, take an old German ferry to Lundy Island and cruise down Coniston Water on the steam launch *Gondola*. As a member of the Nancy Blackett Trust, Sophie has sailed on the Orwell, in the Solent and through the inland waterways of the Netherlands, visiting Middleburg and crossing the Veersemere to Zierikzee. Over the years, she has grabbed the chance to sail yachts to Salcombe, up the coast of Norway and through the Mediterranean, but still loves taking out a small boat in the Lake District.

You can follow Sophie on social media and read more about her exploits on her blog, at sophieneville.net